# How to Prepare
## for Your
# High-School Reunion
### and Other Midlife Musings

Also by Susan Allen Toth

*Blooming:* A SMALL-TOWN GIRLHOOD
*Ivy Days:* MAKING MY WAY OUT EAST

# How to Prepare
## for Your
# High-School Reunion
## and Other Midlife Musings

*by Susan Allen Toth*

LITTLE, BROWN AND COMPANY

BOSTON          TORONTO

FIRST EDITION

All of the incidents in this book are true although
many of the names have been changed.

Some of these essays have appeared, occasionally in slightly different form
and under different titles, in the following publications. They are reprinted
by permission.
*Architecture Minnesota:* "Living with an Architect"
*Harper's:* "Going to the Movies"
*Minneapolis Star and Tribune:* "E. B. White"; "How to Prepare for Your High-
School Reunion"; "My New Year's Resolution: A Shorter List"
*New York Times:* "A Traveler Returns"; "Turning onto Less-Traveled Roads"
*New York Times Book Review:* "The Importance of Being Remembered"
*North American Review:* "Sounds"
*Redbook:* "On Picking Raspberries"; "The Cut-Glass Christmas"; and "Alarms"
Copyright © 1980, 1982 by The Hearst Corporation. All rights reserved.
*Twin Cities:* "A Leg Up in Life"; "Country Reminders"; "Dime-Store Dreams";
"Giggles"; "Good-bye to Garage Sales"; "In Praise of.Minnesota Weather";
"In Search of Quiet Places"; "Moving"; "Reunion: Coming Home"; "Sure,
You Can Learn to Ski!"; "Teachers"; "Up with 'Domestic'!"; "Walking Around
the Lake"
*Vantage Point:* " 'If You're a Writer, Why Aren't You Writing?' "
*Vogue:* "I'll Stay in the Slow Lane, Thanks"

*Library of Congress Cataloging-in-Publication Data*

Toth, Susan Allen.
   How to prepare for your high-school reunion and other midlife
musings / by Susan Allen Toth. — 1st ed.
      p.    cm.
   1. Middle age — United States.    I. Title.
HQ1059.5.U5T68    1988
305.2'44 — dc19                                           87-29816
                                                              CIP

RRD VA

*Published simultaneously in Canada
by Little, Brown & Company (Canada) Limited*

PRINTED IN THE UNITED STATES OF AMERICA

This book is dedicated to the memory of my father,
Edward Douglas Allen (1908–1947):
I have missed him.

# Contents

Contents

# Acknowledgments

I WOULD LIKE to thank three editors: Valerie Monroe, then at *MS*, who suggested I try writing in my own voice and who has continued to encourage me; Anne Mollegen Smith, who as fiction editor of *Redbook* published "On Picking Raspberries," which got me started; and Marcia Appel, who, as editor first of *Twin Cities Woman* and then of *Twin Cities*, said to me with warmth and trust, "Write on whatever you want."

I am also grateful to the people and place of the MacDowell Colony, who twice gave me the quiet time I needed.

# Preface:
# Out of the Parking Lot,
# into the Sea

*WHEN I WAS YOUNG, I saw middle age as a vast dull expanse, something like a big gray parking lot baking in the sun, filled with empty cars, deserted of life, but serving a useful purpose. I certainly didn't intend to end up parked there. In my comfortable midwestern town, middle-aged women led lives that seemed, from my child's view, modest, neat, and suitable as the dark print dresses they wore. They were busy with house and family, church groups, clubs, and bridge; a few had jobs. Most had husbands, equally busy, who drove back and forth to work, mowed lawns and shoveled snow, sat with their wives at football games and took their families on vacations at Minnesota resorts. It all looked quite predictable, uninteresting, and devoid of incident.*

*But by the time I myself reached middle age — a vague boundary, which threatened to begin at thirty when I was twenty but which kept quietly slipping ahead whenever I started to approach it — I realized that this phase of American life had been transformed. Suddenly middle age was quite unpredictable, and full of incident. It had become a midlife crisis, a ritual passage, a transition that was being studied, analyzed, and thoroughly reported. The guides I read told me I was entering a sociopsychological process that sounded disconcertingly similar to the much-publicized steps in grieving, involving denial, anger, bargaining, and acceptance. I was supposed to examine my life, reorder my priorities, and sort myself out. If I followed the process correctly, I would eventually emerge, fit and determined, on the other side — into an old age that had, alas, not yet become fashionable.*

*But of course it didn't happen quite like that. My years from the mid-thirties to mid-forties — a period I've arbitrarily decided to call "middle," followed indefinitely by "upper middle" — didn't seem at the time to lead anywhere much, except older. I didn't sense I was in a charted passage, then or afterward. I kept hoping I was about to coast into a tranquil inland lake, but in fact I seemed to be sailing precariously along a rocky, formidable, though fascinating coast. When I found a harbor, I never stayed very long. Soon I'd start asking for maps no one could find, though the authorities recommended some that were outdated, others irrelevant, a few indecipherable. Then I'd sail out again, sometimes excited, sometimes saying, "Oh no. Not again," sometimes seasick. Now in my late forties, I still feel I'm on board. On the days when I want to stop moving — or when, as one friend said to me, "I've had just about enough of this growth stuff" — I can at least be pleased I have never found myself stalled in a sun-baked parking lot.*

*During those ten years I did try to assess my life, eventually publishing two memoirs about my childhood and adolescence and about my years at college in the East. I also wrote many short personal essays, usually because something happened that made me want to put my feelings down in words. This book is a collection of those essays.*

*The essays cover many topics, more notes for a map of my "middle age" than the map itself. Since these years were a fermenting mix of laughter and heaviness of spirit, some of these notes are lighthearted, some are not. I am temperamentally allergic to most philosophical abstractions and generalizations, so I try to avoid using them. They make me itch, as though grains of sand have fallen into my underwear. When asked to write an essay on "the role of the individual artist" for an arts publication, for example, I immediately heard a clear accusing voice: "If You're a Real Writer, Why Aren't You Writing?" I feel the passing of time in very specific ways ("My New Year's Resolution: A Shorter List"), and I respond to death in terms of particular people I have known — or wanted to know ("I Wish Words Would Help," "Grandmother's Story"). Often intrigued by the meaning of details in my daily life, I tend to see evolution and change in my life even in a consideration of knee socks, though I certainly do not meditate upon knee socks as a regular habit.*

*As I reread this collection of essays, I looked for some unifying themes. (After teaching literature in a college classroom for eighteen years, a few reflexes become automatic.) It would be nice, I thought, to see a cohesive story, with discernible plot and satisfying resolution. What I found instead were loosely defined groups of concerns, reflecting many different aspects of my life: mother, teacher, writer, single woman, wife, in varying order of importance.*

*I could see how much I notice material things — those knee socks, for example — and how guilty I often feel about my attachment to them. As a college student, I was struck by the idiosyncratic genius, insight, and style of Henry David Thoreau. His prose had a lightning crackle, illuminating his paragraphs with bursts of brilliance and making me see myself, and other human beings, in a sudden sharper light. I continue to refer to Thoreau again and again, as if to placate a god I keep offending. But I still haven't learned how to pare down to essentials, burn the refuse of my life, and then live in the infinite expectation of the dawn.*

*I also noticed how frequently I reach back into my past to try to tie it firmly to my present. This, of course, was part of the impulse for my two longer memoirs, but other filaments still keep appearing, tempting me to grab hold and attach them, making more anchoring lines between then and now. Perhaps as I balance in the middle, trying to find a precarious poise between yesterday and tomorrow, I need to feel the strength of some continuous line, like a towrope, that I can hold onto.*

*This collection begins with a group of essays about change and acceptance, coming to terms with who I am now. "How to Prepare for Your High-School Reunion" has a companion piece in an essay, "Reunion: Coming Home," included in the last group. Both were written, many months apart, after I attended my twenty-fifth high-school reunion. In the second group, "Dimestore Dreams," are three pieces about my struggle with possessions: how to value them, how to let them go. The third group, "In Search of Quiet Places," is about looking for, and sometimes finding, havens of thought and silence.*

*During my middle years, I have developed some survival skills. In the section "On Picking Raspberries," I write about coping with various challenges, like men and weather. Mostly, I find, I cope by laughter. In the group "Birthday Balloons," I consider celebrations, often bittersweet, some in the past, some looking ahead.*

*For a long time I felt awkward about calling myself a "writer." It seemed such an august title, earned by the authors I reverently studied in graduate school, as well as by the current eminences interviewed in the* New York Times Book Review. *I envied the confidence of a St. Paul license plate I once saw that announced, instead of numbers, "*WRITER.*" In the section "Watching Out for Real Writers," I detect a certain defensive tone, but I think as the years pass and I do, in fact, continue to write, it will calm down.*

*In the last section, "Coming Home," I move from the fears that sometimes engulfed me as a single woman to the complex though loving negotiations of a second marriage. Three essays deal with my growing sense of connection to my maternal grandmother, whom I never knew, and whose story I hope someday to invent and write. The last piece, "Reunion: Coming Home," is partly about coming home to myself.*

# ONE

# How to Prepare for Your High-School Reunion

# How to Prepare for Your High-School Reunion

### I.

OF COURSE you are already on a diet. All over the country, whether in a Dallas French Provincial bedroom or in front of a pier glass in Massachusetts, your high-school classmates are sucking in their stomachs, flexing their chins, and wondering if a dark three-piece suit or an Empire-waisted, vertical-striped dress would help. We all gloomily know in our well-padded bones that no change in years registers as dramatically as an added fifteen pounds. My old friend Charlie was reluctant to attend our reunion until I reassured him that I'd recently seen his former nemesis, smart-alecky Hank Able, whose wisecracks had pursued Charlie like yellow jackets from locker to homeroom to study hall. "Hank's lost a lot of his hair," I reported encouragingly.

"Huh," said Charlie noncommittally.

"He's been divorced twice," I continued, "and he's been working in the same hardware store in Blooming Prairie for ten years."

"Yeah?" said Charlie, a successful banker. There was an unproductive silence.

"And boy, does he have a paunch!" I added, in a burst of inspiration.

"No kidding?" said Charlie with sudden cheer. "Old Hank's bald and fat? You mean, a *real* paunch? For sure?"

He chuckled with happy malevolence. "Well, I guess you're right. I wouldn't miss our reunion for the world."

The diet probably won't work. At first the reunion seems impossibly far away, probably difficult to organize, even unlikely to happen. When confronted with a slice of double-chocolate cheesecake, you will have a hard time holding between you and the plate the picture of Gloria Doats, radiant homecoming queen. Maybe she's gotten plump, you think hopefully. As the weeks suddenly shrink, and you don't, a kind of passive resistance sets in. "This is me," you tell yourself defensively. "I've finally found myself. I know who I am. No problems of self-identity here. And I don't look bad, either, especially not from this angle, if I stand with my shoulders back." I myself boldly confronted this problem by admitting that I might be carrying a few extra pounds, but if I didn't get on a scale, I wouldn't have to know. So I conscientiously didn't weigh myself for six months before our high-school reunion. The day I came home, I checked the scale and immediately went on a diet. Maybe five years from now, for our next reunion. . . .

The moral is: diet, or don't diet.

II.

Decide what you are going to wear. This has nothing to do with the weather, hot and humid in Missouri, rainy in San Francisco, or chilly in northern Minnesota. No, this has to do with image. What kind of person do you want your old classmates to think you have become? Glamorous, in leather jeans and spaghetti-strap top? Domestic, in madras wraparound skirt? Businesslike, in something dark blue that no one will really notice? Funky, in a bright green sweater studded with rhinestones and cut to the waist in back?

What you wear also says something about how much money you have, and people *will* be listening. Some accessories are more noticeable than others. When Kristine drove a brand-new BMW into the parking lot at our reunion, Charlie and I agreed that it was probably the fastest way for her to get to Iowa from Milwaukee, but still, she might have taken the family station wagon. So if you own a pair of Gucci pumps, leave them at home; ditto your Ultrasuede suit or the Trigère dress you always claim you picked up for a song. (Others may feel differently: Brian appeared at our reunion in white linen slacks and an open purple silk shirt with lots of gold chains twined over his tanned chest. Charlie and I studied him from a distance and decided, in whispers, that it wasn't Brian's fault. He'd lived in California for ten years.)

After going through my wardrobe several times, and studying different effects, I finally packed an old orange linen skirt, much washed, and a plain dark silk blouse. Rather Yuppie, I admitted, what with all those wrinkly fibers, but silk always makes me feel slightly slinky. Besides, when I rolled up my sleeves, I could look casually comfortable.

When Charlie picked me up for the first reunion party, I realized that I was not the only one who had been fussing. Natty in a dark blue Italian wool suit, Charlie kept picking nervously at his tie. "Do you think anyone else will have a tie on?" he asked me. I had no idea. We stopped to get Leonard, formerly a skinny water carrier and now a successful corporate lawyer in New York. Confidence personified, right? Leonard was *not* wearing a tie. But after he leaned in the window and saw Charlie, he said, "Wait a moment," and hurried back to the house. When we arrived at the Holiday Inn, they were *both* wearing ties. Glimpsing the crowd flowing in the front door, Charlie suddenly spied our senior-class president. He hissed at Leonard, "Look at John Bremmer! He doesn't even have on a suit!" In a moment both their jackets were neatly folded on the backseat, covering their discarded ties.

Later that night we all wryly agreed that our best-dressed vote had to go to Ted Guest, who had settled improbably in Key West, and who wore faded Levis low on his hips, a clean white T-shirt, and one gold earring in his left ear. We were all a little jealous of his self-assurance.

### III.

Memorize your high-school yearbook. I tried this while fighting bus-sickness on a rattly, swaying ride from Minneapolis to Ames, Iowa, and the faint vertigo of the trip was an initiation into what was to follow. How would I recognize anyone? Whose name did I need to remember? Staring at a picture of a familiar face long forgotten, I tried to recall how we'd known each other. Were we in the same homeroom? Didn't we both have parts in the class play? Some faces brought back buried memories, and I'd look out the bus window at blurring cornfields and instead see myself crowded into a pizza booth, dancing across a gym floor, or crying softly in the girls' bathroom. Long-ago emotions swept over me like dark waves from a hidden inland sea.

When I arrived at the reunion, I was glad I'd done my homework. Not only had time changed many faces, but new hairstyles, mustaches, glasses, and makeup added almost impenetrable disguises. As I searched for someone I used to know, I tried to impose mentally the black-and-white picture from my old yearbook on top of the blurred image in front of me. When a face sharpened into focus, I was enormously relieved when I could call out, "Candy Sherman!" "George!" "Don't tell me it's Emmy Lou!" If someone knew who I was, I certainly wanted to recognize him or her too.

I have to admit I still didn't like Emmy Lou. It surprised me that old enmities, as well as friendships, hadn't changed much. Looking at Emmy Lou's picture on the bus, I couldn't remember why we hadn't gotten along, but I knew we had never wanted to spend much time together. We still didn't. We looked each other up and down, exchanged guarded greetings, and hastily moved on. On the other hand, I was delighted to see some classmates I hadn't thought much about for years. Though I hadn't heard from Tony since we'd graduated, we immediately hugged each other. When I used to go steady with his best friend, and he with mine, we'd double-dated, and later we'd consoled each other after our different breakups. Now we hurried into a corner so we could sit and talk. From time to time, other vaguely familiar faces would swoop down on us, crying, "Tony!" "Don't tell me it's Susan!" They'd obviously consulted *their* yearbooks too.

IV.

What Tony and I talked about was our lives. What had we done with them so far? What did we still hope to do? To prepare properly for a high-school reunion, you need to decide what to tell about yourself. That means you have to know what's important. Not just bare facts: "I'm a manager at IBM, I got married a year ago, I'm going back to law school, I've been divorced since 'eighty-two, my kids are in school now." No, you have to know how you *feel* about your life. Sooner or later, someone is going to ask you, "So, are you happy?" I usually sidestepped that one. "Well," I'd say, "life has been very interesting. Complex." Sometimes I'd go on to elaborate, sometimes not, depending on how close I felt to the person I was talking to.

What surprised me most about the reunion, I think, was how easily most of my old friends and I *did* talk to each other. After years of separation and silence, we came together with intense curiosity, but we talked less about careers than about changing relations with lovers, spouses, children, and parents. Mostly we wanted to know how others had struggled, how they had survived, and what they had learned. At my high-school reunion, I learned how to summarize my life.

V.

Take some pictures with you. This is not for the reason you think. You do not need to flash snapshots because anyone really wants to see Geoffrey, your life's companion, or Melissa, your affectionate Burmese. No, you must be able to glance surreptitiously at these snapshots in order to remind yourself that you *do* have another life back home. A few hours into the reunion, I was so caught up in former alliances, emotional entanglements, and uncertain friendships that I felt a vulnerable seventeen all over again. By the second day, when our reunited gang gathered for a picnic, I was flirting with Ted as if I'd never stopped, I wondered if I'd ever hear from Tony again, and I worried that my best friend Dee Dee wasn't having a good time. I temporarily forgot that any other place or people existed; all that mattered were old friends, shared memories, lost opportunities, and the strangeness of parting again tomorrow. In the bright sunshine falling through the maples in Brookside Park, years melted away.

When I returned to my mother's house that night, I could hardly remember I'd ever left. I lay down on my old bed beneath a window opening on our backyard, tangled and flowering with the same petunias, impatiens, and pansies that my mother planted every summer. I could smell the last of the lilacs; I could hear the same buzzing hum of grasshoppers singing me to sleep. During the long seasons of my growing up, I'd looked out that window every night before closing my eyes, usually wondering about Charlie, Ted, Dee Dee, Tony, and the others, who had said what to whom, what they secretly thought of me, what I secretly thought of them. I was thinking of them tonight.

Suddenly I couldn't stand being disoriented any longer. I flicked on the bedside light, took out my snapshots, and stared hard at them. The faces of my daughter and the man who later became my husband stared back at me. Tomorrow night, I told myself, I'll be back in a different city, in another house, talking of plans, jobs, and daily trivia that my classmates couldn't know about. I was sad, but relieved. I wouldn't want to be seventeen once more, I said silently to my snapshots. I had struggled hard to become who I was, and I didn't want to go back and do it all over again. Coming home had helped me recognize that, though I would have lots to sort out after this weekend was over.

Maybe, I thought, the only way really to prepare for a high-school reunion is to give yourself plenty of credits for the intervening years. Before you go, write your own report card, the kind you always deserved, with whatever notations seem appropriate: S for Generally Satisfactory, E for Extraordinary Effort, I for Improvement, B+ for The Best I Could Do at the Time, Inc for Incomplete because It's Not Over Yet. Keep it hidden in a mental pocket, next to your pictures, and then, when the reunion is over, hang on to your report card, smile at everyone, and go home.

# A Leg Up in Life

"THESE KNEE SOCKS are all yours?" asked the gray-haired saleslady, barely suppressing a note of disbelief. "Yes," I said with nonchalant dignity, but I surreptitiously patted the pile on the counter into a neater, smaller stack. On top were those luscious part-mohair, part-cashmere, heather-toned designer socks I had circled around for some time before gingerly removing them from the display rack. Underneath I had stashed my more utilitarian choices, socks in solid black, brown, red, and olive green, plus a gloriously loud argyle and a pair of turquoise skinny ribs. I had picked through dozens of socks until I found those that were all wool or all cotton, having become, I realized, one of those obnoxious women who gloat over natural fibers; no wonder the saleslady had been beadily glancing sideways at me for the last fifteen minutes. She probably thought I was going to tuck the mohair-cashmere socks in my bag and run.

"You must really like knee socks," the saleslady said in carefully neutral tones as she folded and wrapped my purchase. I could tell she was a little contemptuous of my extravagance. Perhaps she was storing up this anecdote for suppertime conversation, another example of those crazy rich ladies who have nothing to do but wander through Dayton's and buy, buy, buy. "Do you know, some woman, and she was no college kid either, actually bought seven pairs of knee socks today?" I could hear her incredulously telling her husband. She would have been happier, even complacent, if she'd been able to sell me seven pairs of support hose.

"But I've never really *bought* knee socks before!" I wanted to tell her. "I went through my teens and my twenties *hating* them, I never wore them, I always wore *tights*. Boy, what I could tell you about tights! I mean, I've only just *discovered* knee socks! That's why I'm buying so many, because I don't *have* any, and my daughter's are too small to fit me!" But I restrained myself. I like to think I'm grown up. I no longer always try to justify my purchases to the salesladies in Dayton's.

Walking home, with my huge sack of knee socks, I felt quite pleased with myself. That morning I had suddenly joined a vast legion, an army of knee-sock-wearers, which had excluded me for years. It was only a few hours ago, I thought, when I was sitting on the edge of my bed, wondering how to dress for a two-mile walk in the mercurial Minnesota weather. Too warm, really, for my clingy opaque tights; too cold for sandals; too brisk even for nylons. A chilly October morning called for something else. I looked idly down at my bare legs and realized that my skirt hung far below my knees. Without thinking much about hemlines, I had over the past few years let them fall as they would, simply as they came, whether from a store or garage sale or my cousin Doris. Any length was okay, and most lengths were rather long. Now if I had a pair of knee socks, my skirt would cover the tops. I no longer had to face a knee gap.

A knee gap has not been a major worry in my life. But, like many women, I have always been unsure of my body, not entirely confident or even fond of certain parts of it. For instance, I have never much liked my knees. Ever since an otherwise taciturn high-school boyfriend, who had never before commented on my appearance, looked at my legs in shorts and asked, with tactless curiosity, why I didn't shave my knees, I have felt self-conscious about those knobby bumps. They no longer seem to have hair on them, if they ever did, but they still don't look very attractive to my subjective eye. My legs in general have been useful props to get around with, not objects on which to lavish attention.

When I was dropped from an Iowa small town into the astonishing world of an eastern women's college, all the girls I could see in every direction were wearing knee socks. Natty in knee socks and Bermudas, confidently swingy in knee socks and skirts, they wore what I thought was an enviable eastern costume with ease and grace. But when I tried to imitate them I failed miserably. My knee socks always fell down. Slipping and sliding almost unnoticeably, they ineluctably sank to my ankles. Even pulled up tight for their initial hour of bravery, they looked funny. When I saw myself in a mirror, my legs were truncated and fat, two pink sausages whose casing of socks didn't quite cover my knees, knobs that bulged over the top in an embarrassing display of flesh.

So I discovered tights with enormous relief. In those years, the only girls who wore tights were vaguely Bohemian, early forerunners of the hippies, assorted iconoclasts who also had pierced ears, long straight hair, and book bags. Mostly, though, you knew them by their determined black tights, a funereal note that made even our bright yellow gym suits look more serious. They were the girls who edited the literary magazine, sat up all night in the smoker discussing philosophy, and fell in love with disreputable professors. Although I would rather have looked like the kilted and sweatered girls whose necks were swathed in six-foot scarves and whose knee socks always stayed up, I decided to try for the more accessible world of tights.

Black tights, I happily learned, made my legs look almost thin. Sleekly covered from waist to toe, I felt as though I had been magically pared down to an essential self. As a bonus, I could cross my knees without protruding bareness or sit sideways on the floor, legs snaked at an angle, and not worry if anything improper was showing. Although I never pierced my ears, grew my hair out, or applied for a post on the literary magazine, I turned my legs for four years into what I thought were sophisticated black statements. Then, after college, I lived in California, and eschewed stockings entirely, depending instead on authentically hand-sewn leather thongs, with accompanying chapped legs and stubbed toes. Only when I moved to Minnesota, marooned in my first arctic winter, did I remember the glories of tights. Rebelling against the fierce winds that blew up my fashionable nylons and froze my thinly clad bottom, I pulled out my old black Danskins. They were salvation, cozy and snug, though I suppose they looked a little odd with the fussy suits and double-knit dresses I then affected. On top, I tried to look like a young faculty wife, who was also a responsible, adult teacher herself; below, I was still a near-miss hippie.

Soon after my move to Minnesota, though, the tights people began to blossom in colors. At first I found just a few ballet pastels in dance and athletic supplies, and then I watched with delight as an ever-increasing palette of bright, gaudy hues — violets and greens and deep blues — invaded traditional hosiery departments. Eventually, no longer a faculty wife, I began to experiment with a different wardrobe, casual and idiosyncratic, and an important part of my new freedom became mix-and-match tights. It is daunting to ponder that the vicissitudes in my young adult life might well be charted by a progression of knee coverings, but fate has not always encouraged me to be sufficiently solemn. I began to

13

sprout pink legs with purple dresses, green legs under plaid skirts, burgundy legs with colors burgundy doesn't usually go with. I knew I had achieved a distinction of sorts when a student wrote on his course evaluation, "I don't much like the modern novel, but I got a kick out of Ms. Toth's purple tights."

Tights have served me well, and I have not yet abandoned them for fancier, flightier knee socks. But life goes on, needs change, and the breezes of an October morning blow in new beginnings. Besides, I think I like my body better now. Even swathed in heavy wool, my legs don't look so much like battered, upended bowling pins as I used to think. Not only do I respect them for the steady two miles a day they carry me, but I am grateful for the wide, swinging pleasure they give me on my all-weather walks. My legs, I have decided, deserve the very best. Suitably socked, I love to feel the cool air blow up and around my thighs. Knee socks even make me feel smugly healthy. The nurse-clinician in my doctor's office, on guard against yeast infections, has given me what amounts to a prescription for socks instead of tights. Air circulation, she assures me, blows away bacteria.

I could have told all this to the saleslady at Dayton's, but I'm not sure she would have cared. To her, legs are probably legs, socks are just socks, and tights are immutably tights. But when she folded those gorgeous mohair-cashmere knee socks, if she'd thought to ask, "Is this perhaps your first pair?" she could have gotten several summarized chapters of my autobiography. Panty hose would never have seemed the same.

# Sure, You Can Learn to Ski; Or, Fear and Guilt in the Rocky Mountains

SURE, YOU CAN LEARN to ski. That's what everyone told me, and I believed them. The feminist part of my consciousness said firmly, "Remember how you thought you were a total klutz as a kid? Remember how girls weren't encouraged to do anything athletic, and how you felt because you ran last in the relays and ducked the ball in volleyball that you could *never* do anything in sports? Remember how in your thirties you discovered you loved to swim, hike, and bicycle? Of *course* you can do it!" I believed this admonition. My husband and daughter, avid skiers, chimed in, assuring me I only needed a lesson or two before we took a vacation in Aspen. And another voice, a faint echo of my Camp Fire Girls leader, reminded me that with the proper attitude, life is *always* an adventure. We girls can do anything! You betcha!

But at forty-five, I was not sanguine about skiing. I tend to be a worrier, and I didn't like the idea of falling down. I also tend to be imaginative, which is not nice for a worrier. I could easily envision my treacherous spine, which houses a troublesome disc, jerking angrily into sudden strange positions. Snap, crackle, pop. Could an airplane transport me home on a stretcher? Would I be able to negotiate the rest of the winter on crutches?

Nonetheless, I don't like to admit I can't do something

15

(part of that fierce feminism), and I'm anxious to please my family (part of something else entirely). So I decided to take three lessons at Buck Hill, our local ski school. The first one wasn't so bad. After we moved cautiously back and forth on the ground for an hour, the instructor took our class up a chair lift — he sat with me, since he could see how I felt about this — and guided us down the bunny slope. At the end of the second lesson, however, fate delivered an unheeded warning. At the top of a steep hill, my daughter bounced off the chair lift unexpectedly soon, the chair took a lurch upward, I hesitated a moment, and suddenly the lift swung around, with me still on it, and headed back down the hill. In my bright yellow snow pants and old purple jacket, I was very visible against the white snow. The passing crowds on their way up, much entertained, called out with irritating sameness, "Wrong way, lady!" Nonetheless, to my immense credit, I went back for a third lesson. Ignoring the wild-eyed little boys who whistled past me, I slowly sashayed back and forth down the slopes. At the end of that morning I felt I was ready for Aspen.

But a small hill in Minnesota does not prepare anyone for the Rocky Mountains. Before I left, friends tried to be helpful. One decided she'd better warn me about high altitudes. "In case you begin to hyperventilate, don't just blame it on your nerves," she said. "I woke up in the middle of one night after only two martinis and had to breathe into a paper bag." On the plane into Denver, I read in an in-flight magazine: "High altitudes can cause shortness of breath, dizziness, insomnia, restlessness, headache, weakness, and fatigue. So take it easy. Don't go up to 10,000 feet the first day!" Already hyperventilating, I clutched my husband's hand. He patted me absentmindedly and kept on reading a newspaper report of snow conditions.

At first things looked okay. The sun shone brightly

in Aspen, the white-topped mountains gleamed, and I walked outside the airport, breathing in a tentative way. Then, though the afternoon was fading, my husband suggested that we "grab a bite on the slopes and take a few quick runs." It sounded easy. Almost without thinking, I found myself suited up and waiting in line at a lift.

Buttermilk Mountain is, everyone in Aspen agrees, "a pussycat." "The perfect teaching mountain," local brochures rave, "gradual slopes, great for the beginner." On the lift, I began to take in what was happening. I was actually going up a mountain. The ground was far below, much more distant than I remembered at Buck Hill. I looked straight ahead. By the time I had collapsed onto the second lift, I was wondering whether I'd fall out if I fainted. Just as this thought became stronger, I looked down. "This is the only difficult part, Susie," James said encouragingly. What he was talking about was a precipice, a sheer drop of what seemed incalculable depth, that we were now sailing across on our flimsy, open, slowly swaying chair lift. I counted to ten several times over — I'd forgotten what came after ten — and somehow we made it to the top.

That was what finally settled my career as a skier: being at the top. All around me was a dazzling panorama of mountaintops, a picture-postcard view of unbelievable magnificence. But I suddenly realized at that exact moment I was scared of heights. Not just scared, terrified. I didn't want to be standing at the top of the world, and certainly not on two skis. Turning around, hoping to see something reassuring, I dizzily caught a glimpse of a sign: "Buttermilk Mountain. 9,700 feet." I remembered the warning I'd read in the airplane: don't go up to ten thousand feet the first day. Pointing to the sign, I turned accusingly to James. "But it's not *really* ten thousand feet," he said with an air of innocence. "And isn't

17

it beautiful? We can take all the time we want. You'll want to stop and enjoy the view."

I didn't want to stop. I just wanted to get down. And the only way down was on skis. So I started, back and forth, doing my slow snowplow turns, trying to avoid bumps and the steeper part of hills. Throughout that afternoon hordes of skiers passed me: young, old, all sizes and shapes, even one courageous blind skier with a companion. I kept on snowplowing, back and forth. Every so often, when I thought I'd run a long hill, I'd pause and ask James, "Is it much farther?" It was always much farther.

The Ski Patrol and I finally swept the mountain together. That, in fact, is a line I plan to use: I swept Buttermilk with the Ski Patrol. At the bottom my fourteen-year-old was waiting. "Where *were* you, Mom?" she asked heartlessly. "I've been here for over an hour." My husband patted me happily on the back. "I'm so proud of you!" he said. "You're a mountain skier now! You've skied down a mountain!" "Yes," I said grimly, "but I don't *ever* want to do it again."

Having put my foot so firmly down, on solid ground, I was once more assailed by that part of me that said that I — representing all women, of course — could do *anything*. As I wandered aimlessly around Aspen, browsing in stores and trying to entertain myself, I kept thinking I ought to get back on skis again, like someone who has just fallen off a horse. Passing Aspen Mountain in the heart of town, I could see all the brightly colored insect-people swooping and gliding down its near-vertical slope. I knew I ought to be out there with them. Satisfied skiers clumped by me on the streets, sunburned and triumphant, having clearly earned their après-ski. I began to feel the kind of guilt I'd known when, as a novice Camp Fire Girl, I'd flunked my teepee-fire test by failing to light it with three matches.

My daughter at last came to my aid by getting the flu, forcing me to remain within call — and keeping me off the slopes. One day when she was better, I left our condominium for a walk and found a quiet road leading out of town, not toward the lifts or toward Snowmass or indeed toward any skiers at all. It wound instead up to a pass now closed for winter. Although a few houses clustered in the hills for a time, soon they dwindled and disappeared. Aside from the crunch of my boots on the road, I heard only the faint sounds of melting water and an occasional bird. Passing a nature reserve, I watched ducks splashing in a creek, while a V of Canada geese soared overhead. Up above me the mountains loomed, but now they looked awesome rather than frightening. I admired the pattern of pine trees, the swirls of snow, the bright blue sky overhead. As I hiked and breathed in the clear air — no longer worrying that it was too thin — I took my first pleasure in Aspen. From the ground.

On that mountain road in the bright January sun, I realized my chorus of exhorting voices had disappeared. What remained, I acknowledged with gratitude, was my own, not very loud, but at least now audible. "Actually," it said sympathetically, "just because maybe you *could* learn how to ski doesn't necessarily mean you *have* to. Maybe you're meant to be a walker instead. Maybe you don't *want* to zoom down a mountain." I breathed a sigh of deep relief. No, I didn't want to, and I wasn't letting anyone down — not myself, nor my husband, nor Women In General — if I never got on another pair of downhill skis. I didn't have to plead guilty; I could simply enter a no contest and walk away.

When we finally flew out of Aspen, the small plane dipped and dove among air currents that sometimes almost brushed the treetops. Looking out the window briefly, before I clamped on my Walkman, closed my

19

eyes, and tuned in Mozart, I felt I was once more poised at the brink of Buttermilk, ready to ski down. I fought hard to remember what I had learned: I didn't have to do it again. Once Rocky Mountain Airways landed, I didn't have to barnstorm through snow-covered peaks again either. I thought about the expectations we set for ourselves, the images we value, the fear we discount or pretend doesn't exist. I thought about not having to climb mountains just because they're there. And then, with determination, I lay back in my seat and gently let myself off the hook — and off the mountain.

# I'll Stay in the Slow Lane, Thanks

AS YOU CHURN down the fast lane, splashing water into a showy wake like a small outboard motor, you probably don't notice me. I'm the one on the other side of the rope, the quiet swimmer stroking steadily in the slow lane. As you cycle past with a warning cry of "On your left!" you probably glance once in your rearview mirror. I keep pedaling, but soon you circle the curve and I disappear from sight. Huffing and puffing in a determined sweat, you jog by in the early morning. I'm the walker who has stopped for a moment to watch geese circle over the lake. But if you looked, you'd see a small smile on my face. As a child I read my *Aesop's Fables*; I don't mind being the tortoise.

The smile is not one of derision but of self-satisfaction. I did not learn to love exercise until I was in my thirties, and now I am quite pleased with myself. If years ago you were captain of your high-school girls' basketball team, or lifeguard at the YWCA swimming pool, or the tennis pro's favorite pupil, you wouldn't understand. But perhaps, like me, you grew up in an era before girls were encouraged to develop athletic skills. Before "fitness" was a stylish word. Before health food, aerobics, t'ai chi, and yoga. Perhaps you always struck out in work-up softball and lobbed the tennis ball — if you managed to hit it at all — high over the fence into a busy street.

Perhaps you thought of phys ed class as a kind of public torture. Then you will know why I'm smiling.

I didn't become addicted to exercise until after my divorce. At thirty-three I discovered the world had changed since my college days, and I needed to update my image (a phrase I adopted as less threatening than "total personal overhaul"). As a single parent of a small, active child, I also needed to get out of the house. With a daring that soon becomes second nature to divorced women, I joined a health club. To my astonishment, I enjoyed "working out," at my own speed and in total privacy, on various complicated machines. My increased sense of physical vitality led me to begin swimming a few laps in the health club pool, then walking to work, biking to a nearby grocery store, and eventually enrolling in a yoga class.

Before long, I was hooked. I needed a daily "fix" of stretching, deep-breathing exercise in order to feel sane and at least temporarily tranquil. But my approach to exercise, then and now, belongs to the long-ago girl who slunk to the sidelines in embarrassment when she missed the return that lost the game for her volleyball team. Group sports are still about as appealing to me as group sex: okay for swinging hares, but not for us tortoises. When I exercise, I want to be by myself. I like to set my own pace; then I can listen to my body, check taut muscles, and pay attention to my breathing. My mind, which has been zooming into the treetops, spinning miles away, or bouncing off the walls of a fixed idea, quiets down. It returns to my body; while the exercise lasts, I'm all here.

My refusal to participate in competitive sports is also a refusal to *look* competitive. I want to fade into the background, avoiding comparison and comment. So I have invented my own versions of a tortoise's shell. Not for me are the sleek, shiny, and glamorous outfits that proclaim expertise. I eschew the skintight black shorts of a training cyclist, the let's-get-serious tank suit for swimmers who dive off the high board, the waterproof gaiters and Gore-Tex parka of a cross-country skier who races downhill in her spare time. No, I go into sartorial hiding when I exercise. I cultivate the costume of a rank amateur, someone who — given such an awkward appearance — is doing surprisingly well. When I swim, I wear a respectable but rather baggy old suit, one that gives me the excuse of stopping at the end of a lap lane in order to pull up my straps. When I hike, I roll my Levis to the knees, counteracting the zealous impression of my safety helmet.

As for walking, my favorite exercise, I have developed seasonal costumes that cater to unobtrusive comfort. My well-shod feet might give me away (I'm a sucker for the latest-model walking shoes), but above the ankles I am disarmingly sloppy. My winter outfit is my favorite, assembled after the first frost and then kept in a crumpled roll in a special spot in my closet. Home from work, I can peel off my businesslike skin and appear reincarnated minutes later. From the inside out, I am layered in silk long johns and turtleneck; then a wool sweater and elastic-waist flannel slacks; knee-high ski socks and fleece-lined crepe-soled shoes; and a final cover of down jacket, face mask, hat, earmuffs, mittens, and scarf. The total effect, a cross between rummage-sale shoplifter and Sasquatch, is an impenetrable disguise. Keen to the slightest changes in "cool" fashion, my teenage daughter takes one look and, disgusted, decides: "I can't go out with you if you're going to look like *that!*" Which is, of course, what a private walker prefers, anyway.

Down by the lake, I set out happily on my afternoon walk. In a nylon sweat suit, bright yellow and looking quite new, but crackling in the cold, one of the regular joggers sails by me, with wind-blown tears in his eyes and a bluish white patch on his nose. I continue to steam along, slowly and warmly. Soon, far ahead, I see the jogger leave the lake path for the parking lot and shelter from the icy winds. I wrap my six-foot scarf once more around my neck and pick up a little speed for the next mile. Underneath my carapace, you might be able to see what a turtle looks like when she smiles.

# *Actually,*
# *I Had a Lousy Time*

"AND DID YOU HAVE a wonderful time in Rome?" a friend asks, eyeing my suntan and sighing. She has never been to Europe, and until her kids are through college, she won't get there. During June, while I was in Italy, she spent her two-week vacation helping her aged mother move into a tiny apartment.

Actually, I want to tell her, Rome was having a heat wave, the air conditioner in our room only worked on low, mosquitoes flew in when we tried to get fresh air, and I had a ferocious headache for three days. Besides, it was the end of the trip, and I was so tired of sightseeing I couldn't really focus on all those colossal wonders. I just wanted to lie in a cool bath until it was time to go home. But I don't dare to tell the truth. "Um," I hedge, "sort of mixed." I pause, and then add hurriedly, "Though of course Rome is an incredible city." I certainly don't want to sound ungrateful. "It was just too much to see in such a short time." My friend looks skeptical; I'm sure she is thinking I've obviously become jaded, I don't deserve such opportunities, *she* would see the Coliseum, the Forum, the Pantheon, and St. Peter's even if she had to do it on an empty stomach during a boiling afternoon in a swarm of mosquitoes. I change the subject, and we talk about our mothers.

25

Unless I'm the only one who doesn't always have a good time, those of us who travel tend to stretch the truth on occasion. Perhaps we all suffer from some residual guilt at our privileged status. Let's admit it: most travelers have time, money, and a sense of adventure not available to everyone. Even backpacking students, who furiously deny belonging to a tourist class, are still rich in time and freedom. So our privilege makes us feel we ought to enjoy every minute of our travels — or at least enough of the minutes so we can report later, in summary, "Yes, we had a wonderful time."

I *hope* to have a wonderful time. Part of my pleasure is planning, unfolding dog-eared articles, doing modest research in the library, lurking in bookstores and making surreptitious notes, poring over maps and plotting itineraries. For weeks before a trip, I read at night in *The National Trust Guide to Country Houses* or *The English Country Church* or *Haunted Places of Britain,* so excited I sometimes toss and turn, sleepless, hours after all my maps have drifted to the floor. But of course such planning means that I hope I will see not just Stonehenge, but perhaps the lesser-known stone circles nearby, with maybe a side trip to Longleat the same day. I can't bear to think of missing the best extant example in Dorset of a medieval abbey church in the Perpendicular style, and I decide maybe we could stop there on the way to Lyme Regis, where then we could go out in a boat and walk along the coastal path before tea on the promenade.

Of course I forget that it may rain. That it will *probably* rain. That I will have jet lag for several days, spend at least one night wishing I hadn't eaten both trifle and apricot mousse for dessert, undoubtedly have a monthly migraine, and maybe, before long, desperately not want to go anywhere and do anything for a whole afternoon. All these human frailties conflict with my expectations of myself as the Ideal Traveler, filled with energy, determination, and just plain zest. Zest, alas, isn't programmable.

Sometimes fate simply deals a bad trip. On a recent summer extravaganza, my husband and I learned on our second day abroad that two of his grown daughters had been in a car accident. We talked to the doctors and nurses, were told not to come home, debated what to do, decided finally that, given the bedside attendance of mother and other siblings, we would remain where we were, though poised to leave if necessary. But transatlantic calls, family complexities, and just plain worry made the trip a performance, rather than a pleasure. We saw some unforgettable sights, did our best to enjoy ourselves, yet had to report at the end, "Well, it wasn't exactly a wonderful time, because . . ."

It's hard for me to say "lousy" partly because I travel with someone who scarcely knows the meaning of the word. My sunny-tempered husband doesn't fret when the baggage is lost, isn't alarmed when the hotel can't recall our reservation, drives with aplomb through rush-hour traffic in Athens. Mosquitoes don't bite him, and when I am wilting in the heat, he takes off his shirt so he can bask in the sun more fully. So if I start to grump and grumble, I have a very different view of reality countering mine. When my friend asked him how he liked Rome, he said, "Great!"

My husband thinks I'm responsible for our marvelous itineraries (which, in fact, I am), and he praises my planning abilities to the (always blue) skies. As I start to think about our next trip, I tend to ask myself how I can top the last one. So I find myself facing three sets of expectations: my own expectations of myself, what I decide are his, and those I imagine of our friends and relations who understandably envy our opportunities. They add up to the necessity of a Fabulous Trip.

What I am learning, slowly, is that those expectations

27

are bugaboos more fearsome than rainy weather, mosquitoes, canceled reservations, jet lag, or sight-seeing overload. They leave no room for error, weather, mood, or change of heart. So I am trying to cut them down to size, small enough to fit into an ordinary traveler's suitcase. Meanwhile, as I'm paring away, I'm practicing a new kind of response to "How was the trip?" With flat honesty, I remark: "Well, it went pretty much okay." Or, "Could have been better." And, though I'll have to stand in front of a mirror a long time before I sound unashamed: "Frankly, if you want to know, I could hardly wait to get home." In my own traveler's bill of rights, I'm putting in the undeniable right to have a lousy time.

# TWO

# Dime-Store Dreams

# *Dime-Store Dreams*

I WISH I weren't so fond of my possessions. Last night when my daughter overturned a pizza on her new carpet, I saw the red smears of tomato sauce as an irreparable wound. Just because once a friend dropped a borrowed book in her bathtub, I'm uneasy when I lend someone a new book — or a vase or bicycle or even a rickety slide projector. When I left a new pair of shoes on an airplane, I was depressed for two days. The fact that I remember them so vividly — bright green leather, wide and comfy, the last pair in the shop — is itself depressing. I scold myself, recall the biblical verses about laying up treasure on earth, and reread my Thoreau.

Perhaps it all began with the dime store. I hadn't thought of dime stores for years until last July, when I revisited the resort town where I spent my childhood summers. I noticed that on Main Street nearly all the old stores had disappeared. The granite bank had turned into a dilapidated real estate agency, and the venerable department store had a new false front embracing video rental, hardware, and a beauty shop. Only the bakery and the Ben Franklin store remained. "Hey," I said to my husband, "there's the old dime store!" Suddenly I realized how funny those words sounded. I never use them now. I go to Snyder's Drugstore, Target, or Nel-

31

son's Office Supplies for the things I used to buy at the dime store.

"We called it the five-and-dime," my husband said nostalgically. "What did we buy then for a dime?" And, interrupting each other, we were off, walking the aisles of our memories, picking up model airplanes, pincushions, stationery, pencil boxes, and pocket screwdrivers. The dime store had clearly held an important place in both of our small-town lives.

Ames was big enough to have had two dime stores, Ben Franklin in the small business section near the college campus and Woolworth's downtown. I had to ride a bus to shop at Woolworth's, so I knew Ben Franklin much better. Of all the stores on the street, it was the most appealing and accessible to a young child. Although I could ask for empty cigar boxes in the corner pipe shop, or rummage through the scrap box at Carter's Printing Press, I knew I didn't belong there. I was intimidated by the gleaming drugstore, with its shiny tile floor and vaguely medical atmosphere, and girls never went into Abe's Men's Store. Ben Franklin, however, welcomed browsers, even young children. We had our pennies for bubble gum and candy, and as our allowances grew with us, we came with nickels and dimes. We walked and looked, pondered and coveted — and sometimes, after much consideration, we bought.

The Ben Franklin dime store was just the right size. I could always find exactly what I wanted. Candy was up front, near the cash register, where Mr. Odebolt, the owner, could keep a sharp eye on small hands. Toys were in the back, near pots and pans, rolls of oilcloth, and a few bolts of fabric. School supplies, whose index cards, paper clips, and stamp pads spoke of neatness and efficiency, lay across glass dividers from frivolous party goods, gaily colored napkins, candles, and sugary cake decorations. Though the store held only three long aisles, Mr. Odebolt kept some goods beneath the counters, and at the rear, he sometimes descended a dark staircase to a mysterious cellar full of unpacked boxes.

Everything a child could want was in the dime store, all within the realm of possibility — if I saved my allowance, did some baby-sitting, or helped Mrs. Sweeney with her fall cleaning. I didn't covet mink coats, Chanel suits, or Helena Rubinstein cosmetics, any more than I could have wanted a down pillow, Wedgewood china, or a silk nightie. I only knew enough to want what was in the dime store.

Although the dime store catered to everyone, I thought of it as primarily a woman's world, filled with romantic images. Some toys appealed to both boys and girls: puzzles, kites, colored squares of clay, Slinkies that uncoiled down a flight of stairs, paddles with little rubber balls attached by an elastic string, tiny turtles with painted backs, and goldfish in glass-globe tanks. Boys bought cap guns, matchbox cars, and rubber snakes in the dime store, and their fathers occasionally came in for bottled ink, a new bandanna, or Scotch tape. But mostly men shopped for *their* domestic needs — tools, nails, ladders, paint — in the hardware store.

Women did their dreaming in the dime store. As a child, I was enchanted by the cosmetics section, so extensive it unrolled down half an aisle, with soaps, compacts, lipsticks, and perfumes, glistening promises of Maybelline eyes and a Woodbury complexion. That aisle was filled for me with exotic scents, like Evening in Paris and Muguet, and luscious colors, Fire-engine Red nail polish or Peach Blush powder. I looked and saw promises. Studying the paraphernalia of beauty, I thought if I owned emery boards, cuticle sticks, cuticle oil, cotton balls, nail polish, and nail-polish remover, I would have the hands of a princess. Cold cream, foundation, and rouge would turn my cheeks into roses, and a rubber-tipped eyelash curler might make my eyes appear as large as Elizabeth Taylor's.

On the other side of the cosmetics counter lay sewing supplies. That, after all, was what lay ahead for girls. In eighth grade we learned to sew in Home Economics, while the boys made lamp bases or pipe stands in Shop. I hurried down to the dime store whenever I ran out of thread or needed a zipper. I wasn't as fascinated with that counter as with cosmetics, but I did admire the papers of pins, in neat pierced rows; the shadings of muted color in the spools of thread and embroidery floss; the small precise tools of thimble, hem ruler, needle threader, marking wheel, and darning apple. At the back of the store, near the rolls of oilcloth, I pored over the Simplicity pattern book, with its infinite wardrobe laid out in glamorous sketches.

At Christmas, when I was shopping for my mother, I even took pleasure in the kitchen section. I admired the green glass vases, white milk pitchers, salt-and-pepper sets shaped like cats and dogs, and gilt-edged teapots. The stacked dishes, like grown-up doll sets with innumerable cups and saucers and plates and bowls, seemed in their bright newness as if they'd never have to be washed. Metal silverware, can openers, apple corers, and paring knives, lined up neatly in their separate compartments, sparkled like clean surgical instruments. From a dime-store point of view, housekeeping looked like fun.

All the major holidays were marked with cards, candy, and paste-up decorations. I looked forward to the painfully sweet selection of just the right book of snap-out Valentines, which usually turned out to be the same book everyone else in sixth grade bought too. I liked Easter egg dye with decals that always smeared, green plastic grass to put into green and pink baskets, small yellow cotton chicks the size of my thumb. One November I brought home a large paper turkey that opened in honeycomb folds.

But at Christmas the dime store outdid itself. I temporarily deserted Ben Franklin then for the larger Woolworth's downtown, which, like all Main Street, was decorated outside with garlands and red tissue-paper bells. Inside Woolworth's was also transformed, its scuffed wooden floors and dingy walls overpowered by aisles filled with shiny glass balls, red and green foil, rolls of lustrous satin ribbon, colored wrapping paper, gaudy tinsel ropes, and twinkling electric lights. My sister and I were each allowed to pick out one new ornament every year, choosing among metal reindeer with sprinklings of gritty silver dazzle, gold-crowned angels with gilded harps, sequined Christmas trees, red-and-white-striped candy canes. While we pondered, we could hear in the background Christmas carols pealing loudly from a radio in back, while whiffs of fresh popcorn drifted down the aisle from a crackling machine by the front register. Sometimes we splurged not only on a box of popcorn but on a few chocolate-covered cherries, heaped on a counter together with peppermint candies, maple-sugar leaves, real sugar canes, and Whitman's chocolates.

Christmas shopping in Woolworth's was an expedition that required much reconnoitering, consideration, and a final last-minute exhilarating plunge into the crowds. At last I was free to spend frivolously, picking out just the right gift — I hoped — for each person I cared about. I remember cut-glass bowls, yearly sets of measuring spoons and Evening in Paris perfume for my mother; stationery for my sister; and for my friends, paper dolls, barrettes, and bath-oil beads. Where I paused longest was at the gift counter. I would have liked someone on my list for a painted china shepherdess, an ashtray in the shape of a garbage can with lid, a large red flocked plaster dog, or a rhinestone-studded miniflashlight on a key ring.

But *anyone*, I knew, would like a miniature. Miniature replicas of animals and objects, usually made of china but also of glass, wood, or even plastic, were a dimestore exclusive, and my sister and I hunted them passionately for years. Not long ago, cleaning out my mother's house, I found what was left of my miniature dogs (my sister specialized in horses, dishes, and cats). Even today, committed as I am to ridding myself of junk, I could not bear to throw away a half-inch big-eyed cocker spaniel, a one-inch gallant collie, and a bean-sized dachshund. Right now I am looking at them, nonplussed, wondering where to find a child who might treasure them too.

I was not alone in my love of miniatures. In dime stores we explored on summer car trips, my sister and I always found a counter like the one in our own Woolworth's, filled with other tiny animals, houses, furniture. Was it a way for Americans to own things they couldn't have in reality, or which, if full-sized, would take up far too much space? Miniatures certainly were within my sister's and my price range, though we couldn't buy many at once. We had to save some of our carefully hoarded "travel money" for other souvenirs, also from the dime store: folding sets of postcards, birchbark canoes, china dishes with "Bismarck, N.D." imprinted in gold script. Whenever we drove down the main street of a strange town, we pestered Mother to go slowly so we could look for a dime store; "Stop! Stop!" we'd shriek, anticipating with beating hearts the treasures we might find in each new Woolworth's or Ben Franklin. As soon as we saw the familiar sign, Mason City or Glenwood or Sioux Falls seemed a little less strange; after we pushed open the glass door and scattered in search of souvenirs, we felt completely at home.

For me, growing up, America was dotted not by churches, libraries, or even schools, but by dime stores. They came into my life at just the right time to help mold my character. Born just after the Depression and raised to save my pennies, I had modest but strong desires to own things. The dime store encouraged those desires and catered to them. And, embarrassed as I sometimes am by recurrent acquisitiveness, an underlying American disease as hard to eradicate as malaria in the tropics, I remember the enticing color, glitter, and gleam of my childhood dime stores — and it is hard to regret they took me in.

# Good-bye to Garage Sales

MAYBE PART of my midlife crisis is no longer wanting to go to garage sales. I don't know; Gail Sheehy doesn't mention garage sales in *Passages*. On weekends I drive, blinkered, past all the tempting signs, my nine-year-old daughter bouncing with excitement as she reads them aloud, stressing the exclamation marks: "Sale Today, 10 to 4, 3541 Fairmount," "Garage Sale in Alley, Turn Here," "Estate Sale Today, 9 to 5," "Bikes, Toys, Antiques!" Most of the time now I make excuses: we're late, she'll miss Disney, I don't have any money, I'm too tired. But those aren't my real reasons.

When did my heart stop leaping at the hand-lettered sale signs? I used to love all forms of domestic rummage, garage sales, estate sales, basement sales, tag sales. In the first few years of my marriage, and then later when, divorced, I bought my own house, I avidly visited those sales for furnishings and gadgets. Why should I buy a fancy new waffle iron at Dayton's when I'd see three or four, perhaps a bit rusted or needing a new cord, but perfectly serviceable, in one Saturday afternoon? Did I need a new rug? In some dank basement I'd be sure to find a threadbare Oriental, a sturdy braided rug, or at least a room-size carpet with lots of wear left that I could use until I found what I really wanted. Poring over cluttered tables, I'd unearth creamers, can openers, rolling pins, candles only slightly burned, flowerpots, canisters, knives, screwdrivers. Happily I'd count out a few dollars and hurry home with my treasures: all this for only $4.92! How clever I felt as I unpacked four twisted-stem wineglasses and set them on an empty shelf, next to a soft blue, slightly cracked vase, at least twenty years old and certainly almost an antique.

Perhaps part of my problem is that now my house is full. All my walls and floors are covered, my shelves filled. I have vases in every size, pitchers for syrup and cream and water, baskets and boxes to hold paper clips or matches or pencils, candle holders in bright colors and flowerpots from China, Mexico, and Red Wing, Minnesota. I have no room to put anything else. As I clean, halfheartedly dusting under, over, and around my daughter's papier-mâché owl, decorated shells, and clay sculptures, I think of friends who live a few blocks away, in another world, with only a few rugs on a polished floor, a few oak chairs, and a sofa. No magazines, no newspapers, no clutter. Just shining surfaces, plants, and a few carefully selected paintings on the wall. When their son was little, he was not allowed to bring home junk, artwork, or projects from other people's houses. They met him at the door, examined his bulging paper bag, and dumped his watercolors, pebbles, and plastic spoons in the trash can outside. They never went to garage sales.

Now, as I look about me and wonder how to change my life, I think perhaps I should have a garage sale of my own. Clear it all out! Sale! 10 to 4! Thoreau, whom I idolize, was stern on this point: he would order me to sweep out the trivia of my life, eliminate excess, and pare it all down. Why should I need more than one pitcher or one vase? Perhaps no pitcher, no vase. I look about me and despair. But after so many years I have become attached to my secondhand possessions. I think of them as having histories, and only part of that history is mine to dispose of. When I pour milk from an old ivory-colored pitcher, crazed with wrinkles but still solid, I wonder whose table it first graced years ago, when it was elegant and new. It is a simple pitcher, with gently curved lines and an unobtrusive embossed decoration. Did it give its first owner pleasure? Was it on a farmhouse table, an everyday accompaniment like salt and pepper, or was it in the small parlor, with her "best things," of some quiet spinster in an old neighborhood here in St. Paul? I do not want it to pass into uncaring hands.

That is part of my problem, too. I look at the objects now at garage sales and see stories behind them. Most sales are organized and run by women, youngish or middle-aged, in their twenties or thirties, now or once married, usually with children. Old women do not have garage sales. They no longer want to part with what they own; when they die, their daughters or nieces will hold an estate sale and dispose of it all in one day, a lifetime's accumulation parceled out to strangers who wait in line at the door.

What do women in their middle years want to get rid of? I look at the jumbled heaps on the card tables in front of me and wonder. Many of them seem to want to get rid of wedding presents. Easy to identify, they have a tarnished splendor: the hammered copper tray, the silver-plated chafing dish, the two-foot white china lazy Susan, the nesting Mexican ashtrays, the banquet-sized brocade tablecloth. No one ever bought these for herself. Some distant relative, or a well-meaning neighbor, or an old college friend of her mother, gave the bride that lazy Susan ten years ago and she hasn't used it once. Was it a gesture of goodwill, or merely a thoughtless choice? Did the giver imagine for the bride a life of formal entertaining, polished silver, and dainty tea sand-

wiches? What does that long-ago bride think now, as
hauls the piece from its wrappings in the attic or ta
it down from the high shelf, blowing the dust, wrinkl.ng
her nose? Had she ever wanted that imagined life of
ease and gracious living? Is she giving up any dreams
along with the linen tablecloth? Does she think guiltily
of Aunt Hilda, who had spent so much of her small
income on the chafing dish, or is she just glad to see it
go? Now does she have, at last, a clear view of what she
wants? Something simple, utilitarian. Something she can
*use*. A marriage that *works*.

I come to a dead stop in front of the handiwork, the
cross-stitched tea aprons, the embroidered bridge cloths,
the crocheted pot holders, knitted afghans, or the dain-
tily worked dresser scarves. I hold up a small purple
linen guest towel, monogrammed by hand in ivory
threads. "Mother," my daughter says admonishingly, "are
you going to *buy* that?" I may. I know it needs to be
washed, I may not get around to ironing it for months,
and then it will probably hang unused on the rack while
my guests thoughtfully dry their hands on the dirty,
crumpled family towel instead. But I cannot bear to see
this careful embroidery tossed, rejected, among old ashtrays and soiled stuffed animals. Some woman spent
hours on that towel. I know; I once embroidered a pair
of men's shorts, for a Valentine's Day joke, and in anxious hours I still stab away at a large needlepointed pillow I began eight years ago. It is slowly filling up, the
white spaces erratically but steadily disappearing like the
days of my life.

I look at that purple guest towel, and although those
are not my cream-colored initials, they might be. I can
see myself, older, alone, propped by pillows upright on
a narrow bed, peering nearsightedly through my glasses
at the square inside my embroidery hoop. Or I see myself, that other woman, walking wearily into a crowded

room, hot and noisy, television blaring, the pop of beer cans and the crunch of crackers. Everyone is watching *Dallas* while I sink for a few moments into an easy chair, unnoticed, and pick up the handiwork I do each night. I like to be here with my family, and doing this embroidery gives me an excuse. Or was I once a young, engaged girl, working on this little towel with anticipation, love, and perhaps a little fear, planning my hope chest? It is not so long ago that we all had hope chests of one kind or another. Even if this embroidery was only time-consuming labor, nothing but numbing stitches, a mindless way to pass long afternoons and meaningless nights, it is still a record, even an unhappy one. Some woman cared enough, or wanted not to care enough, to sew part of herself into every tiny stitch, so very tiny her eyes must have ached as she sewed. Now, like her history, it has been carelessly discarded. Of course I am going to buy it and take it home.

But I do not need any more hand towels. I have so many. I own several afghans, one for each bed and sofa and one folded over my favorite chair in the living room. I don't use tablecloths. I have a drawerful, all embroidered or hand-decorated, folded neatly in my dining room, but it is so much easier to pull out my wipe-off place mats. I have dresser scarves on two dressers, but they collect dust, and I know I should get rid of them. But to whom? How?

Depressed, I move on to the rack of old clothes at the back of the garage. Now I am angry. I can salvage one small purple guest towel, but I have no intention of trying to do anything about this sad, bedraggled collection. I don't mind children's clothes; Jennie and I rummage together quite happily to find usable jeans, T-shirts, and sweaters. But the others! Faded miniskirts, stained ruffled blouses, pink polyester pantsuits, baggy green sweaters, fashions just "out" enough to look awkward rather than antique. Men's pants with shiny seats, shirts with frayed cuffs, jackets whose padded shoulders have sunk lopsidedly. Such clothes, hanging still with the impress of someone's body like dismal ghosts in this dark garage, seem so personal they embarrass me. They should not be recycled. They should be decently buried. At least don't sell them for profit, I want to say to the woman behind the cash box, banging my fist on the card table. Call the Goodwill, the Salvation Army, the Veterans Auxiliary! I can tell I am getting crotchety; just part of my midlife crisis, I try to reassure myself.

Jennie brings a small china planter in the shape of a horse to the table and sets it down. One leg is broken. "This is only twenty cents, Mommy," she says pleadingly, "and I'll pay it back as soon as we get home from my piggy bank." I look at the purple linen guest towel in my hand and nod. The woman behind the card table looks at Jennie and me and smiles pleasantly. "Nice day today, isn't it?" she says. And indeed the sun is shining brightly, despite the cold currents swirling over the cement floor from a late October chill. "Have you had a good day?" I respond, equally politely. "Oh yes," she nods, "you wouldn't believe how much we've sold since yesterday. You should have come early then, when we had so much more." Jennie looks at me reproachfully. I glance at what is left, the tablefuls of junk, the rack of clothes, and wonder how this woman can bear to haul it back into the house, stuff it in the attic, or somehow find room for all these oddments in corners of shelves and closets. I want to tell her about Thoreau's idea of a bonfire. Instead of auctioning off someone's effects at death, he said, we should burn them in a purifying ritual. He observed at such an auction how "the neighbors eagerly collected to view them, bought them all, and carefully transported them to their garrets and dust holes, to lie there until their estates were settled, when they

43

will start again. When a man dies," Thoreau concluded in a melancholy pun, "he kicks the dust."

But I suppress the impulse to quote. I have to take my daughter, china horse planter, and purple linen towel home now, and Thoreau would certainly not approve of any of them. Or of me, for that matter. I put the linen towel on the front seat.

On the way home I glance at my watch. Still a few hours left of daylight. I'll put on my dirtiest jeans and clean out the garden, preparing it for its winter rest. I'll pull out the frozen zinnias, prune the raspberry bushes, and cut the last parsley. My growing compost heap can be dug back into the soil next spring to enrich the garden. That thought cheers me. Soon it will be too cold to work outside, and then perhaps I can start on the basement. I haven't really touched it for five years, and it's time I sorted through that unsewn fabric, those old appliances, paint cans, and rusty skates. I'll pack everything into garbage bags and label them. I'll pile them in a corner. I won't look at them again. I'll pretend they're already gone. And maybe next spring I'll find the courage for a sale of my own. But I'm not sure.

# Sounds

I AM SITTING on my back porch this stormy June morning, thinking a little about Thoreau, because my beans are climbing high, but thinking even more how quiet it is. Robins are loudly singing in the lilacs, so perhaps the rain will hold off a while longer. Except for the robins, a droning airplane overhead, and a faint constant humming of traffic two blocks away, it is quiet.

As I sit here, admiring my beans and marveling at the birds, I realize how seldom my life holds so little noise. Most of the time I hear a whole orchestra of competing sounds, all tuning up together: my daughter's lilting inquisitive voice, dynamite exploding on *Tom and Jerry*, a buzzing timer for the pizza, the pounding of a dishwasher. Perhaps because this is such a quiet cool morning, a breeze blowing in from the lilacs, I think of another writer, Sarah Orne Jewett, and the silence of life in her Maine fishing village. I can close my eyes and hear the few sounds that broke her silence: bees in a summer field, sheep bells, the scrape of a boat down at the landing. Fewer, and more soothing, noises than mine. As I sit now in this squeaky metal chair, wishing I could hear waves washing against the Maine coast, I am awash in the undertow of the sounds in my own life.

Years ago, when I first read *Walden,* Thoreau's chapter on sounds opened my ears. But I was struck then, and I am still amazed, by the difference in sounds that constitute his world and mine. Not only did he live by a country pond while I live on a crowded city street; but, more important, he was a defiantly lonely man, and I have chosen to link my life to others. On a winter morning he listened to the booming of frozen ice on a winter pond, while I and my daughter wait near the screech of rusty skates sharpening at Cliff's Hardware. But I do not mind the noises there. We talk to a neighbor waiting in line behind us; Cliff asks about the weather outside; his wife rings up two mousetraps at the cash register; my daughter chatters with excitement. It is a cacophony I am not sure Thoreau would know how to interpret.

I know he would hate my machines. So much of my noise is mechanical: on hot summer days, through open windows the buzzing and throbbing of clippers, mowers, edgers. In winter, the high-pitched grunt of the snowplow. Every Wednesday, sun or snow, the ravenous growl of the garbage truck. But these noises are reassuring, they tell me things are working, the system continues. I do not want to bury my own watermelon rinds or walk two miles to my office in knee-high drifts. Inside my house I listen for the comforting underground hum of things working too: the refrigerator gurgles loudly, the dehumidifier gasps and stops and gasps again, the furnace clicks and then roars softly. I am glad to hear them. I do not wish to haul ice onto a back porch, scrape mold from my cellar walls, stoke a fireplace with logs.

Now that I think about how much I depend on that

background of mechanical noise, the hums and whirs that together form a continuo like the ominous Machine in E. M. Forster's prescient tale, "The Machine Stops," in which everything eventually breaks down in apocalypse, I become a little nervous. I realize how sensitively I am tuned in to my machines, as much perhaps as Thoreau to the hourly thawing of ice on Walden Pond. I am always on edge for the sounds that indicate something is going wrong. A clank in the basement: did the furnace just go out? The pipes may freeze before the repairman gets here. Hundreds of dollars. Maybe a new furnace. Two thousand. Any strange metallic noise means trouble, money, time, worry. I am used to the rejecting thump of my overloaded washer, which, having announced its irritation, usually turns itself off. But when last week a loud *thrunk* made my kitchen floor vibrate, I rushed down the stairs. A fuse had blown, smoke hovered over the machine, the Maytag man might come tomorrow morning if I stayed home from work but he might not, a load of sopping clothes to the laundromat. Even little noises can make my heart sink. Click, click, click; the dishwasher can't quite make it into the rinse cycle. It is two months out of warranty. Another repairman, another wait, another big bill. I try not to think of Thoreau now. I know what he would say: "Our houses are such unwieldy property that we are often imprisoned rather than housed in them."

Thoreau and Jewett could listen peacefully to water, the murmur of a pond, the wash of a tide. I listen to water too, but indoors the sound of water is ominous. Something must be managed, taken care of, watched, turned off. A washing machine churns; soon after its water sloshes into the tub, I will have to dump the clothes in the dryer, sort, fold, put away. Faucets gush hot water into the bathtub: the tub mustn't overflow, Jennie mustn't burn herself, I will have to stay close to the bathroom, clean out the tub afterward. Sometimes the toilet runs, wasting water, asking to be jiggled, coddled, fixed. I do not like to have my toilet talk to me. The worst water sound I have heard recently was a slow rush of waves in my basement, a sound of something emptying, something else spreading, filling up. The water heater had broken, flooding the floor. Where was the turnoff valve? What would happen to the gas connection? How could I mop all that up? How soon could I get a new heater? How much would it cost? What would I do with the old one? I hate the sound of water indoors.

But perhaps this morning I can hear raindrops, if I wait on the porch long enough for the storm to break. Meanwhile I can listen to the swoosh of maple leaves in the big drooping tree in my front yard. They rustle so gently, like the lapping of waves, that I am lulled, here in my chair, to lean back against the wall and dream once more of Maine. Soon, though, I must get up. I have to drive before lunch to the grocery store; we are out of milk, eggs, lettuce, paper towels. Instead of listening to wind in the leaves, I will have to attune all my senses to my Dodge Dart. It is old now, eight years, which in human terms must be a hundred and two, and it is breaking down insidiously, one joint at a time. I am no mechanic, but I have had to learn how to listen to my car. Perhaps the way I have tuned myself in to that rusty purple Dodge is a paradigm of what sounds I have had to make most important in my life.

How relieved I am when my Dodge is working: the motor throbs; the turn signal rat-a-tat-tats; the washer fluid squirts with the splat of spilled juice on my windshield. Then I sit happily at the intersection, as the motor vibrates steadily and loudly: we will make it to the end of the freeway, we will get where we're going, we may even get home again. But most of the time I am poised, tense and alert, for the sounds of things going wrong. I know some of them. Who could miss the whine of a dying battery, the heavy *thwap* of a flat tire on pavement, the gunfire of a bad muffler? I even know more esoteric sounds: the loud dry scraping of a leak in my power-steering fluid; the squeak of a bad shock-absorber gasket; the faint *thrump-thrump-thrump* of a faulty heat-riser valve. That last one was an auditory triumph, showing how sensitive I have become. My friendly mechanic didn't hear it at first, he thought maybe my choke spring was bad. But I told him to keep very still as I drove around the block: *thrump-thrump-thrump* when I accelerated. Yes, he said finally, he guessed he could hear that. It was probably the heat-riser valve. Hard to get at, two days to get parts, could I leave the car sometime when convenient. It's never convenient. Someday my Dodge will drop a vital organ, and I may not be able to turn, or stop, or keep steering straight. My life may depend on how carefully I listen to what it's telling me. So I listen hard.

As I sit here, thinking about my old Dodge waiting in the driveway with patient malignance, the telephone rings. In the few seconds it takes me to reach the phone, I realize that someone I don't want to talk to is going to be on the line. Someone wanting something. The telephone rings so insistently: I want, I want. I want to sell you aluminum siding, ask your advice, tell you what my lover said last night, find out tomorrow's assignment. It is a demanding noise, like the others, wanting not only time and money but also affection. Yet once in a while there will be a voice on the other end I need to hear; so I answer.

Most noises in my life do demand something, I say to myself irritably as I sit down once more on the porch.

I can seldom just listen to anything for pure pleasure. Now I sense Thoreau standing behind me, cutting through self-pity to the obvious, always unbearably right. Haven't I chosen to live this life? Couldn't I tear out my telephone, sell my car, heat water on a wood stove, and wash dishes with tallow soap? Couldn't I live on the beach in Mexico, join a commune in Vermont, move to Arizona with a tent and a horse? I could do any of those things, I suppose, except I don't choose to.

And yet, I would say in some confusion to Thoreau, I have some sounds in my life that bring me joy. True: I do not often get to listen to a hooting owl, the scream of a hawk, the sweet peal of a church bell vibrating through the woods. But, finely tuned as my ears are to the mechanical continuo of my civilized life, I am also tuned in to human sounds. You would never understand them, for they are a kind you never knew. I think of my daughter.

When my daughter is home, our house is filled with excited cries, laughter, questions, or, as she puts it, just plain "chitter-chatter." It resounds with her delighted whoop as she runs through the sprinkler, the songs she sings lovingly to her dolls, the serious conversations she has with wounded stuffed animals. It reverberates with her jarring whine, that dissonance like a violin string out of tune and played without rosin. She has many tones, though I seldom analyze them or sort them out consciously. I hear them instead like my own heartbeat, as familiar and as essential to my own well-being. Sometimes when I have to try to pay attention to her voice and to the noises of my machines at the same time, I become cross and distracted. But I concentrate on her sounds first: she, after all, speaks my name, and my machines do not.

Many of the sounds of love in my life are indistinguishable from the sounds of responsibility. Perhaps that is why now that she is gone for the day, I can feel myself unwind so completely. For a little while, I can shut off that part of my hearing apparatus. Some of the ways a parent listens are not so different from constantly being alert for an ominous clank, or gurgle, or click. The soft padding of small feet in the hall at night wakens me like a cap pistol; it means trouble, maybe only thirst, perhaps an upset stomach, a fever, a nightmare. Trouble has many sounds. Muffled crying: hurt feelings, anger, and a need for reassurance. Most terrifying of all, what I think of as the blood cry: a shriek that means something has been cut, hurts, is bleeding. As I run, much faster than for a flooding water heater, I do not know until I get there whether it is a cracked skull or a torn fingernail. In those moments, I am always amazed how that cry has cut through me like a knife.

As I sit here on the porch, remembering with a shiver the last time I heard that blood cry, I feel a touch of cold. I notice that I no longer hear the leaves. The wind has died, dark clouds have covered the sun, the birds have stopped singing. A murmur of distant thunder: a summer storm is coming. I must go inside and shut the windows. Then to the grocery store. My brief moment of peace is over. But I will have other moments; as I rise, scraping the metal chair against the cement, I think one last time of Thoreau, my machines, my daughter. I would like to tell Thoreau about the most peaceful sound I know. It is one I can listen to every night. Just before I put out the lights and go to bed, I walk into my daughter's room to cover her shoulders and to see if she is sleeping soundly. She almost always is, curled into a nestling shape, her chest rising and falling with the faintest of breaths. I stand there for a short time, hearing only the soft sounds of her sleep, a gentle sigh, in and out, in and out. All other noises drop away, a knot of twisted melodies that now falls harmlessly to the floor. I have distinguished most of them, but I cannot tell exactly how they are all wound together. Yet as I listen to my own breathing in a counterpoint to hers, I know I am standing in the still center of my life.

# Moving

FOR WEEKS afterward I dreamed I was in the basement of my old house. Sometimes I was frantically sweeping, scrubbing, or trying to scrape peeling paint from the cement walls. Sometimes I was simply staring into a dark, cobwebby corner, so close I could smell the dank dirt in front of my nose. But often I was tugging at a mildewed cardboard carton. Where the carton had stood was a damp spot on the cement, crawling with black beetles. I didn't know what I was going to do with the carton. I hadn't opened it for so long I had forgotten what was inside. In my dream I knew, despairingly, that behind me and in other rooms, in countless forgotten corners, lay more damp spots and more cartons. I would never be able to get out of my basement.

I know some people *like* moving. Last fall at a party I met the wife of a computer executive, so successful and ambitious that he leaps upward from job to job. They had moved ten times in fourteen years. Before I could express adequate commiseration, she said cheerfully, "Oh, but I love it. I like going to new places and meeting new people. And I enjoy fixing up houses, decorating, and arranging furniture, and moving things around." Her husband joined us and added, "She's not kidding. Even when we're settled, I never know when I leave the house in the morning what I'm going to find when I come home. Once I walked into what had been the dining room in the morning, only to find that in the last eight hours it had become a study."

I smiled in a glazed way, murmured something polite, and escaped to the buffet to smear more blue cheese on my celery stick. I didn't think the executive's wife and I would have much in common. I hate to move. In fact, I hate change of almost any kind, which may be why for seventeen years I've taught at the same college, had my teeth cleaned every six months by the same dentist, and cooked Malt-O-Meal for breakfast every winter morning. Occasionally I indulge in a few novelties, coloring green streaks in my hair or learning how to cross-country ski, but I have never learned to like moving. Over two decades I have changed houses three times, and each time I swore would be the last. A year ago, when I moved from a house with ten years' accumulation, I realized that moving had gotten harder, not easier, as I had grown older.

When they heard I was getting married, several of my friends said smugly, "Moving will be good for you." I liked to think they were merely wishing me well on my change of life, but in fact they were commenting on my happily cluttered rooms, ceilings hung with mobiles, and overflowing bookshelves. "One of these days," a less tactful friend had told me months before, "you're going to run out of space." I myself, in dark moments, thought I might die an eccentric old lady, found after unnoticed days lying among piles of newspapers and unanswered letters. So now as I wrapped plates in newspaper and stacked books in heavy-duty grocery bags, I tried to tell myself how good this was for me. Like having my teeth filled, or jogging two miles with a headache, or diving into an icy lake on a rainy day.

To hearten myself, I tried to recall the example of Callie Cooper. I only met Callie once, in a crowded backstage room at a local television studio, where we were both waiting for momentary interviews, but I may never forget our exchange. Making awkward conversation, I must have asked Callie, whose bravura paintings I had seen splashed on the art pages, what she was doing just now. I think I expected she might describe some new project or show. Instead she said briskly, "Getting ready for my sale. I'm having my forty-fifth birthday next Saturday." "You are?" I echoed, in some confusion.

Callie explained. Every five years on her birthday, she had a sale. She wanted to clear everything out of her life and begin anew. To do that, she not only had to get rid of all her old possessions, but she needed fresh capital. "So I give a huge party," she said. "I put a price tag on everything in my apartment. Absolutely everything. I tell my friends to bring *their* friends, and I let the word out as far as I can. It's quite a bash, and when it's over, not only am I down to the bare walls, but I have a nice little nest egg." I was in awe. Immediately I pictured my own crowded house, my beloved books, my favorite red leather pumps, my antique wicker sofa. "Everything?" I echoed again, this time unbelievingly. "Even your clothes?" Everything, Callie assured me. Once you started keeping something out of the sale, you had defeated its purpose. I nodded politely, but already I was thinking of other ways out of this dilemma. Maybe you could put an extra-high price on the things you really wanted to keep? A hundred dollars on a pair of used red shoes?

When I moved last year, I found it hard to get rid of anything. Raised in a thrifty Iowa family, I learned early how to use up, make do, and save. Now I had to face an accusing array of objects that were "still good," as my mother used to say when I held up a pair of jeans or shoes I wanted to replace. I also had to face what each object represented. Many of my excess things spoke to me reproachfully about good intentions gone sour. Some had to do with cooking: a yogurt maker I'd used only a few times before I discovered I really didn't eat that much yogurt. A steamed-pudding mold for the one Christmas a friend had asked me to bring plum pudding for dinner. Shiny barbecue skewers, when I thought I might start barbecuing, though I never did. A genuine French quiche pan still in its box, from the time I devotedly watched *The French Chef*. Stacks of tablecloths and hostess aprons, reminding me how I used to picture myself as constantly entertaining.

And how could I admit to myself that I'd never sew again? For years I'd made many of my own clothes, until a hectic schedule, combined with my discovery of secondhand stores, finally destroyed my incentive. What should I do with my cache of fabric? I'd been so pleased with each purchase, a paisley Liberty print from London, a silk from Amluxen's vintage days, a bright terry cloth from a Minnesota Fabrics bargain table. Should I also throw away all my old patterns, tracing paper, and spare zippers? Saying good-bye to the young wife and mother who approached gourmet cuisine and sewing with eager intensity, I saw her disappear down a time tunnel I had walked through without noticing it.

Other oddments reminded me of past hopeful images of myself. A pad of watercolor paper and some paints, from a summer when I thought I'd develop my "artistic side." Stacks of sheet music, purchased when I determined to practice the piano an hour every day. A calligraphy set, never opened, when I somehow imagined I needed a new hobby. A tennis racket, though I hadn't played in years. A bicycle rack, which I had never figured out how to attach to my small Toyota, and which I had thought would encourage me to bike at scenic places like Stillwater on quiet Sunday mornings. Now I had to admit I rarely had quiet Sunday mornings, and when I did, I didn't spend them in Stillwater.

So moving made me face up to my past and present, what I did now and who I really was. As part of disburdening myself, I next had to come to terms with Olive Mae Harrington. Olive Mae, a formidable and autocratic woman who ran my moving sale, had definite ideas about what everything was worth. Not much, she pointed out. When she and her crew of elderly assistants began sorting and arranging my china, pie pans, and linens, I overheard disheartening fragments of their evaluations. "What do you think about this lamp?" Olive would ask a helper, in a discouraging tone. "Oh, I don't know. Ten dollars?" the helper would reply, deferring to Olive's superior knowledge. From the kitchen, where I was packing my spices, I wanted to dash into the living room and snatch it from her hands. TEN DOLLARS? For a marble base and silk shade, both of which I'd acquired on the second floor of the City of Paris department store in 1964? For my very first purchase for my first apartment? TEN DOLLARS? Perhaps it was the cold objectivity of Olive's voice that hurt me most. To her, of course, it was just a lamp, out of style and with a chipped edge.

As a veteran estate-sale shopper myself, I knew she was right. Low prices were essential. Yet as I overheard other fragments — "Does anyone wear this kind of thing anymore?" "No one will buy those. Better put them in the dollar box." "That's cracked." — I still wanted to rush to the defense of many of my underappreciated and undervalued possessions.

What cured me at last were the antique dolls. They weren't mine. After looking over my discards, Olive had haughtily informed me that *her* followers expected more than *this* at her sales. So she would have to bring in "a few other things." I didn't pay much attention to what "other things" might be until someone's entire collection of dolls arrived, and Olive demanded I clear out an upstairs bedroom so that they could be properly displayed on my floor-to-ceiling bookshelves. Olive and her chief assistant conferred for hours with the dolls behind the closed bedroom door. During the afternoon two doll experts arrived for paid appraisals, but at different times, since neither was supposed to know the other was coming. "Dolls are a cutthroat business," Olive explained. "Everyone wants a first crack. But someone could undervalue a doll and get a friend to come and buy it for her tomorrow." When the experts had gone, she was clearly pleased. "The kewpie is really rare," I heard her say gloatingly to her assistant. Late that night, just before leaving for my new home across town, I asked my husband to peek with me inside the doll room.

In the glaring light from an overhead bulb, we stood in dismayed silence for a few moments. "Wow," I finally said. My husband let out his breath forcefully. In front of us the dolls were arranged like small corpses laid in a morgue, tier upon tier. A few were life-size, which made the likeness even eerier. Most were decidedly old and damaged, worn, cracked, or faded. Several, with unpleasant expressions or distorted proportions, were downright ugly. Others, now "collectibles," originally had been cheap prizes at carnivals. I glanced at a few price tags: no ten-dollar bargains here. Forty, eighty dollars and more. A few were marked six and seven hundred. I gingerly touched one of the life-size babies. "That's creepy," my husband said. "Let's get out of here."

I looked around at the dolls, once toys, now something else entirely. No children would play with any of them again. They would be displayed on wire stands — Olive was selling a few of those too — and probably covered with glass bubbles. My husband was right; they did look dead. Dead because they were not used anymore, only venerated. Things you don't use are transformed, I thought to myself, and I don't think I like what they become. The prices for these dusty relics were still whirring in my head. Why had I been fussing about that ten-dollar lamp? Value was not only relative, it was weird.

Suddenly I wanted to get out of the house quickly and not come back until the sale was over. I was ready to part with everything. I hoped it would all go to people who could use it, and I no longer cared what Olive would sell it for. Good riddance to bad rubbish, I thought, remembering a defiant childhood jeer. Afraid my impulse might not last, I tugged at my husband's hand. "Come on," I said. "Let's get out of here and leave all this stuff behind. On to the new house."

"And we'll stop at Lund's and get some fresh flowers to celebrate," James said. I think he knew I was finally ready to move. Shutting the door of the room firmly, without looking back, I took his hand and went down the stairs.

# THREE

# In Search of Quiet Places

# Country Reminders

THE JULY SUN beat on our heads as my nine-year-old daughter and I walked slowly out of the hospital. The nurse had warned me to have her back in twenty minutes. "Let's just take a walk around the block and see what we can see," I said encouragingly to Jennie, taking her hand firmly. But I wasn't hopeful. Cars whooshed by a few feet from us, billboards loomed at the corner, and with each hot breeze, disintegrating cardboard and dented beer cans blew into the gutters. How could I cheer my flu-ridden child and remind her that a world outside still existed?

Walking past a deserted parking lot, we saw, wedged in the cracked concrete, weeds flourishing and alive with white and yellow flowers. "See those flowers, Jennie?" I asked eagerly. "Why don't we pick a few to take back to your room?" Jennie's listless face brightened. "Could we?" She hesitated. "You've always said it's bad to pick wildflowers." "Yes, but this is okay, here they're just weeds," I reassured her. Together, slowly, we toured the parking lot.

"Look, Mom, see these pretty daisies. Do you think we could pick some of those? And maybe some of these blue ones?" She moved on to the next clump. "Let's see how many different kinds we can find," I suggested. Soon Jennie was happily darting about the parking lot, her weakness almost forgotten. No longer a disused, ugly urban waste, the parking lot had become a field of flowers. A few I recognized: the soft spiky purple of clover, the determined sunny faces of dandelions, the bright red-orange of devil's paintbrush. Others were mysteries, tiny yellow petals clustered on a gray-green stalk, white miniature daisies, even a kind of bluebell that drooped gracefully over a broken piece of iron railing. Some blossoms were so delicate they spilled from our hands, shaken from their stems. Others stained our fingers with milky juices as we broke them off. Sniffing carefully, Jennie even found a few blooms with faint, odd fragrances. As though we were botanists making rare discoveries, we exclaimed to each other and gathered our weedy bouquets, while below us, on the busy street, cars rushed by and acrid exhaust drifted on the hot summer breeze.

Later, back in the hospital room, the flowers didn't last long. But we both had been cheered by our brief expedition. Our world did not consist merely of these gray concrete walls, tile floor, or plastic-upholstered chairs. Outside somewhere was an irrepressible force that bloomed with yellow and white gaiety even in a drab, forgotten city corner.

Now when I am in the country, I often remember that parking lot. It made me begin to think in new ways about myself and my environment. I wonder why, as a confirmed city person, I go to the country at all. What do I find there that I need? My "country" is not what other Minnesotans usually mean when they talk about "getting away." I don't head to the North Woods or Boundary Waters. Addicted to faucets, flush toilets, and a socket for my electric typewriter, I seldom pitch my tent in the wilderness. For me, "country" might mean a long weekend on a friend's farm, where, with the dew from sumac branches splashing my face, I warily climb the snake-infested bluff behind their house. "Country" might be a sun-baked hour in a wild raspberry patch near a lake cabin, or a shady, winding path through scraggly woods of birch and sugar maples to a clearing of maple-sugar vats.

But I still need to get to my country, tame as it may be, in order to keep living with some degree of sanity in a city. What is it, I ask myself on some of my modest excursions, that I want to be reminded of? The answers that occur to me are not, alas, deeply philosophical. General concepts from essays on man and nature always dissipate in my mind like passing clouds. I do remember a few phrases and images from *Walden,* but *Walden* is an unusual book; unlike many philosophers, Thoreau seizes a reader by the scruff of her neck and forces her to *see.* So he is the writer who walks along with me on a country road or through the hillside sumac. Somehow he listens, even if skeptically, while I try to explain why I'm out here.

First, I tell him, I like to be reminded about dirt. At home I struggle against it, sweeping bits of mud from the kitchen linoleum, vacuuming dust balls under the bed, and scolding my daughter if she doesn't wipe her feet. Even though my house never looks like my neighbor's, neat and squeaky clean, I aspire. Spots are sponged, puddles mopped, ashes emptied. We use lots of soap at our house — hand soap, bubble bath, dishwasher and laundry detergent — all to get rid of dirt. But in the country, dirt takes over. Earth, mud, and just plain dirt are part of the natural order, and even the most compulsive cleaner has to succumb to the inevitable. It is, in fact, a relief to stop trying. When I follow my friend's husband into his barn, I wear a dirt-encrusted old jacket from the row of stained and tattered garments that hang by his back door. We slop through the trampled mud near the barn door and enter the old, dark, pungent-

65

smelling building. Inside I duck beneath cobwebs, kick aside some mucky straw from the end stall, and climb the uneven boards to look at a new calf. In the milking barn everything is spotless, but here "cleaning the barn" only means shoveling out manure. No one ever comes to the old barn with soap and water. Joel and Sheila have more important things to do. They live peaceably with dirt all day.

Before supper that night I take my usual stroll along the county road that runs in front of Joel and Sheila's farmhouse. No rain fell today, and the hot afternoon sun has dried up all the moisture of the morning. As I walk along the dirt shoulder, I kick up small clouds of dust. I rather like its acrid smell; a paradox, I think wryly to myself: dirt that smells clean. No lingering odors of garbage, sewers, gasoline, exhaust. Just drying hay, blowing weeds, and earth baking in the sun. I am walking on the edge of a great open oven, and the dust smells as comforting and as eternal as the loaves of bread that sometimes fill my city kitchen with their yeasty aroma. Tonight the gentle dust, blowing in wisps, reminds me of summer nights in my Iowa childhood, long auto trips in the burning sun, endless roads tunneling between cornfields, and lazy afternoons in a Girl Scout campground. It is part of a natural order and has nothing in common with the mop, dustpans, and vacuum cleaners that stand guard over my city life.

Not only do I like to be reminded about dirt, but I learn in the country about the difference between mess and richness. One recent spring morning in northern Minnesota, I found myself on a different kind of country road, this one the narrowest possible lane leading from a hidden lake to a county highway a few miles away. No fields of hay or corn here, no open spaces at all, no dust. All I could see on either side of the shaded road was a green tangle, woods and underbrush forming a dense wall that stopped abruptly at the ditch. As I walked down the lane, swatting at mosquitoes that lurked in every wavering shadow, I peered into the dark woods. I couldn't see far. White fallen birches, moss-covered decaying logs, vines and bushes all twined together, like a giant heap of jackstraws, so that someone standing a few feet from the road would have been screened from view.

I marveled at the way it all fit together. Everywhere I saw infinite complexity, all held in a balance that could nonetheless absorb the next fallen tree, the newest pile of leaves. I thought about my own life and my desperate struggles to keep it in order. In my house, it seemed to me, mess walked in every door at all hours of the day: grocery bags, *New Yorkers*, my daughter's art projects, discarded sneakers, a damp beach towel. I didn't see my mess as richness. But perhaps it was.

As I walked farther on this cool, cloudy Minnesota morning, I began to lose track of where I was. The woods looked much the same behind me, next to me, and over the next rise. Under an impenetrably gray sky, the narrow road marched on and on. I glanced at my watch. I had been walking for almost an hour, but since I had often stopped to examine flowers, or to watch a stray frog, I had no idea how far I had come. Eventually, I knew, I would see from the top of the hill a concrete highway joining my dirt road in a definitive perpendicular. But meanwhile I could just swing my legs freely, feel my muscles pull to the task, and walk through a slight ache to the next rise. It had been a long time since I had measured distance by the swing of my legs; always, in the city, I knew how far I had already walked and precisely how far I had to go.

As I stretched my legs, I could also stretch my eyes. I had forgotten how liberating it felt to be able to see into a disappearing distance, where the trees gradually shrink and the sky bends down to meet the land. All around me was space, a magic carpet silently unrolling as I stepped along it. After years in the city, I was used to seeing only a few blocks at a time at best, and usually I found myself staring at a row of buildings that cut my perspective like a drop curtain. Worse, my vision often simply terminated in the rusty bumper of the car ahead of me. Here in the country, simply because I could see as far as the natural slope permitted, I felt as though a restraining load no longer weighed me down. Thoreau nudged me; his sometime friend, Emerson, had once said, "The health of the eye seems to demand a horizon. We are never tired, so long as we can see far enough."

My companionable thoughts ceased abruptly when I began to hear a disturbing sound, a far-off hum of traffic. In what I call the country, traces of the city are never very far away. Although I may have been let out on a day pass, I know I have to report in custody again as soon as the sun sets — if not today, then tomorrow, or the day after that. Meanwhile, I must clear the dull film from my eyes, so I can differentiate the subtle shade of green in the next thicket, and take the deafening cotton from my ears, so I can trace the descent of a dive-bombing mosquito. When I return to the city, for a short while I will be able to see and hear clearly, as I do here.

So, I find myself telling Thoreau, perhaps I do know why I need the country after all. What I visit are places marked on the peripheries, and sometimes even ordered, by the works of man. I do not pretend that I have penetrated the heart of wildness that Thoreau knew. But my country borders on his, and is an outlying part of it. Perhaps that is why I resent bulletins that report pipelines destroying delicate tundra, strip-mining tearing open Appalachian hills, or pollutants pouring into the Great Lakes. I don't want motorboats on wilderness lakes, or fancy resorts built on untouched mountains. I want to save farmland, wetlands, dirt roads, lakes, woods, and ponds. Even if I don't live in the country, I need to know it is *there*, just as Jennie and I needed to know in her air-conditioned, antiseptic hospital room that unsown flowers were blooming in an untended parking lot outside her window.

# Walking Around the Lake

🌸 PEOPLE IN MAINE clamber along the rocks —
I know, because I've clambered there too. In northern California, they hike in the redwoods or near the shore. Growing up in an Iowa college town, my friends and I liked to wander over the sprawling campus lawns. In St. Paul, where I lived happily for twenty years, I sometimes strolled along the banks of the Mississippi, peering among trees for signs of the water below. But in south Minneapolis, where I live now, I walk around the lake. And though I miss my old neighborhood and the grandeur of its nearby river, I don't ever want to live far from a lake again.

"Walking around the lake" is a peculiarly Twin Cities preoccupation. When new friends ask me where I live, and I tell them "a half-block from Lake Harriet," their faces often light up and they say, "Well, someday we'll have to walk around the lake together." Others invite me to circumnavigate whatever lake is closest to them — Isles, Nokomis, Como. Why? What are we all doing out there? What turns us into lake fanatics, appearing in odd garb in all kinds of weather, chugging around the lake in icy cold or weaving among fair-weather crowds on a summer night?

Note: we are *not* jogging. Although I've tried it, I hate the jerking and bouncing, the rigorous up and down, the heavy thud of my Nikes on the pavement. The land-scape blurs, and my thoughts jangle. Jogging interferes with meditation, and I think that is the main reason why I walk. When my nerves are kinked into knots, and my mind is whirring, I need to stretch, slowly and carefully.

Setting out in a rhythmic stride, back and forth, I remember our high-school drama coach's advice: pre-tend someone is pulling you by a string tied to your hips, and glide. Swing from the hip and glide, swing from the hip and glide. Saying this instruction over and over, and trying to follow it, I relax. Dum-dee-dee-dum and glide: my walking takes on a kind of hypnotic effect, as when I fall into a successful cross-country ski step and my body moves along the slick grooves as if on silent, greased bearings. A doctor once told me that walking and cross-country skiing were repetitive activities that soothe the reptilian part of the brain. She didn't explain what that was, but later, heading around the lake, I happily pic-tured myself as an ancient lizard, something descended from prehistoric monsters, drawing on millennia of wis-dom and survival. Now when I walk I sometimes think of a tiny snake, curled in a corner of my brain, sunning itself in the pleasure of my reptilian pursuit.

What do I think of when I walk? I wish I could report that I solve complex problems or compose whole para-graphs. In fact my mind refuses to function in a logical way on walks. But somehow, as I swing and glide, things get untangled. And as knots gradually loosen, I can see different strings lying there — perhaps watched over by that benign, sun-warmed snake — and I feel better about picking them up again. I may even see how I can weave them into a different pattern. Sometimes images rise in my mind, as in dreams, that I can follow later to see where they lead. Almost always I feel that cobwebs have been swept away by the cold wind blowing across the lake, or burnt to a crisp by the fierce midsummer sun, or gently pulled down by the persistent plucking of the first warm breeze of spring.

The seasons matter in a special way to those of us who walk around the lake. We salute and mark their passing, as if we were a private audience for nature's theatrics. We can't ignore the weather: walking every day, one has to confront what is out there. But weather in Minnesota changes so quickly, altering whatever it touches, that the lake reminds me that time is moving and changing too. Subzero temperatures don't seem so prolonged, nor summer heat so impassively permanent.

When freezing air touches the lake in fall, forcing warm mist to rise from the water, I watch every day for the ice to form. Meanwhile snow falls into the dark water, disappearing silently even while it clogs the sidewalks and drifts under the trees. The ice begins slowly, foamy crusts at the edge of the shore, battered, blown, and at first dissolved by the waves lapping against its edges. But one morning I see that a delicate rind has covered the whole periphery of the lake, except for the small ponds a few ducks and geese keep open until impossibly late. Signs go up — "Dangerous! Thin Ice" — and I wait eagerly to see if the lake will freeze hard and solid into a skating surface before the first heavy snowfall can cover the ice. On just such an evening a few years ago, I drove all the way from St. Paul in order to skate from one end of the lake to the other in the rapidly falling dusk. Although I passed a few tiny tents lit by ice fishermen's lanterns, I was otherwise alone in the dark, listening to the click of my blades on the ice and watching the far glow of houses on the surrounding hills.

In spring the ice melts slowly, but a walker notices that the thaw is moving closer each day. If you stay inside during the slow approach of warm weather, you're sure it will never come, because outside the window nothing seems to happen. On the street and sidewalk all you see is old snow and melting slush. But around the lake, you notice changes. Small gray puddles form on the surface of the ice and sparkle in the sunlight. Slowly the puddles grow larger, and near the shore the ice begins to look thin and uncertain. On the sidewalk, an obstacle course of sinkholes and muddy sloughs, walkers grin at each other in commiseration as they leap from one solid footing to another, carving out new routes in the banks and dodging the splashes of runners who refuse to detour for either water or walkers. Gradually the ice melts completely, the ducks and geese return, and suddenly the grass is green once more — squishy underfoot, soggy in spots, but alive.

In summer and fall a walker has all kinds of wildlife for company, from an occasional turtle or snake to birds, squirrels, waterfowl, and rodents. I anxiously watch the duckling broods who appear in spring, since by late summer many of these large families have shrunk in size. What predators got them? That large white cat I saw lurking in the reeds? Other ducklings, hatched quite late, look so young and unskilled even in late fall that I wonder how they'll ever manage to migrate. Yet they eventually disappear with the rest; maybe they grew up very fast at the end. In July, when the water is inviting at my favorite swimming beach, a muskrat patrols the shore most afternoons just before dinnertime. At least, I *think* it's a muskrat; a horrified walker once stopped me and, pointing, gasped: "Do you see that rat? He must like the fancy garbage in the sewers around here. Ugh!" Ever since then, I've tried to take my swim at noon.

I'm not a birder, but many walkers are. I stopped once on a sunny fall day next to someone who was transfixed by something far out on the lake. He saw me, turned, and said, excited, "Do you see that whistling swan and two goslings?" Nearsighted, I squinted and just barely focused on their long necks. Other walkers

73

have pointed out the flamboyant coloring of a pair of wood ducks, a bald eagle soaring overhead, and smaller, unusual songbirds I would otherwise have missed. Once, pausing to marvel at the hordes of mud hens who cover the surface of Harriet for weeks in the fall, I had a spirited discussion with two other walkers who'd stopped at the same spot. How many birds could we see? Spread over the lake in the daytime, the mud hens are too scattered to be impressive, but at night or in severe weather, huddled in a floating convoy, they look like the population of a substantial town gathered on a football field. Counting them would make a nice civic contest, we agreed, like guessing the number of peas in a glass jar.

Warm weather brings out varied human specimens as well. We winter walkers take a superior attitude toward those who only appear when they no longer need face masks, knee-high boots, and six-foot woolen scarves. As a stream of joggers passes me on the first sunny afternoon of spring, I mutter to myself, "And where were *you* last week?" Regular walkers recognize each other, sometimes nodding, exchanging a few pleasantries, or even falling briefly into step. I'm sure many of us wonder about the life stories, occupations, and even health histories of the regulars we never get to know. Is that elegant, white-haired woman married to the younger man who always walks with her, or is he possibly her son? Why does that middle-aged portly man walk around the lake in midafternoon, when everyone else is at work? Why doesn't he ever smile? What has happened to the valiant stroke victim who so carefully made his way around the lake all spring? Is he recovered — or gone?

But although I enjoy watching other walkers, or studying the crowds on summer beaches, I like the lake best when I have it almost to myself. Living a crowded and often noisy life, I am happy to take my mind off its leash and let it waft over a tranquil mile of water. Walking around the lake, I often try to focus on emptiness, the space stretching toward the opposite shore and the sky overhead. Here, without buildings, roads, cars, or hurrying people, I feel the quiet. One of my best walks last year was during a heavy summer rain, one that didn't stop for hours. Armed with a sturdy umbrella and vinyl slicker, I walked determinedly into the wind, reveling in the splash of rain over my head, watching the sheets of rain drive across the water, waiting for the dramatic rumbles of distant thunder. Passing no one, huddled into my slicker with my head down, I was wonderfully alone. When I returned to my house, where the phone was ringing, the television was on, and doors were slamming, I felt as if I'd just come back from a long trip.

Lake Harriet is not the Antarctic, but I thought of Scott and Amundsen once last winter. My daughter and I were keeping each other company — it was just past twilight, and I have a city dweller's uneasiness at solitary nighttime walks — on a bitterly cold, windy evening. Although we started in the usual counterclockwise direction, suddenly I looked at the empty stretch of ice and said, "Why don't we cut across it?" It was an eerie walk. A light snow began to fall, and the wind whipped the flakes about in the growing darkness. Toward the middle of the lake, thoroughly chilled, we realized that we could barely see ahead of us. Lashed by the wind, blinded by the snow, ears heavily muffled, we looked around to the shore behind us. We could only glimpse fragments. It was so quiet we sounded strange when we spoke to each other in quick cold gasps. The far shore seemed miles away. All that was real was our immediate world: the crunch of light snow over ice underfoot, the whistle of the wind, and the sharp cold. For a moment I could imagine we were trudging across polar wastes, with only snow for a horizon and endless ice everywhere. When we reached the shore and climbed up the banks to the safe sidewalk, I was relieved. But I was also exhilarated.

Sometimes — for a few minutes, with my eyes closed — Lake Harriet even seems like Maine. When a storm is coming and the wind is whipping up, I like to walk along the windward shore and watch the waves. Near the bandshell, where a retaining wall and dock offer some resistance to the water, the waves lift and crash, with a sound like surf on the rocks. Landlocked in Minnesota, I get lonesome for the ocean, and that sound helps. On windy, stormy days, Harriet is transformed; she is no longer a tame, citified lake. As the sky darkens, white-winged sailboats fly for shelter, swimmers scurry like ants, and most of the joggers hurry home. But a few of us walkers who are indoors hear the signal in the rising wind and hurry for the front door instead. The lake is calling. Grab your coat and get your hat, leave your worries on the doorstep. It's time for a walk. And when the lake calls, I listen.

# Mud Races

ALTHOUGH the next night I dreamed I was struggling through sloppy waves of thick brown goo, I am still not sure of the significance of the Cheshire County Fair mud races. Writers often find meaning in what seem like unremarkable incidents, perhaps repressed anger in a spilled cup of coffee, lost optimism in an endless game of tic-tac-toe, or renewed confidence in a Fourth of July parade. On my bookcase is a framed quotation from Philip Roth: "We writers are lucky: nothing truly bad can happen to us. It's all material." I think the mud races are probably material, but I don't know what for.

I had never seen a mud race until the summer of 1987, and if I hadn't been an artist-in-residence at the MacDowell Colony in Peterborough, New Hampshire, I might never have gotten to one. Living first in Iowa and then Minnesota, I had of course heard of stock-car races, demolition derbies, tractor pulls, and hog-calling contests. Even as a child, however, I had never wanted to watch them. Ignoring the grandstand, I looked instead at winning quilts and cakes, ate cotton candy and hot dogs, took a few scary rides, tossed losing nickels in glass saucers, and went home.

But when Dan, a printmaker, mentioned at breakfast that he was driving to the mud races in late afternoon,

I eagerly asked if I could go along. Adrian, a composer; Glenda, a novelist; and Mark, a poet, wanted to come too. Evenings at art colonies can be very long. After working all day, or even just reading alone in my studio, I didn't usually feel like returning to my silent space. So I often found myself agreeing to — even searching out — activities I would protest wildly at home. I propped myself on the floor for poetry readings and attended taped concerts of very modern music. Sometimes I sat on a hard-backed chair in the stuffy TV room and watched rented movies. Always chosen by artists who had cars to go to the video store, these movies tended to be either depressing foreign films recommended by everyone's friends in New York, raunchy comedies with rock stars, or dark dramas reeking with violence. One night I watched all of *Pee Wee Herman's Big Adventure*. I was longing for Fred Astaire or Jack Lemmon, but I didn't have a car. Tonight, someone was renting *Southern Comfort*. Without inquiring, I thought of bourbon, potbellied sheriffs, blood in the swamps, and quickly decided on the Cheshire County Fair.

I also liked the sound of "mud races." What I vaguely pictured was a muddy track, maybe a foot or two deep, with stock cars roaring through it, whizzing and splashing, and crowds cheering. Action, speed, excitement. There was also something reassuringly real about all that mud. At art colonies, no one talks much about their cats, gardens, jobs, best friends, spouses, lovers, or children. This is probably as it should be. Still, after being at MacDowell for two weeks, I needed a little down-home mud.

Barreling along the New Hampshire roads in Dan's new Mazda van, all of us were in high spirits. We traded memories and compared names for cotton candy (the Iowa, and therefore proper, label): Glenda had known it in Australia as "fairy floss," Adrian from England remembered "candy floss," and Mark thought of "spun sugar." Looking out the window, watching the dark dappled woods and occasional villages flash by, I began to fall into my traveling mood as a child, when I had a sense of an unknown treat waiting at the end of the road.

Perhaps, I thought, going to these mud races would bring back the neon glamour of traveling carnivals in Ames, Iowa, when I stared at swarthy women wearing large gold earrings in their immorally pierced ears. Or the State Fair Midway in Des Moines, where strippers gyrated in satin bikinis outside a tent called Pussycat Parlor and where slick-haired barkers called seductively, "Hey, missy! Come on over here! Three balls for a dollar and a prize every time!"

Maybe the mud races might become an essay about returning to simple pleasures. At MacDowell, I had a hard time not thinking of possible essays. My Pivot, a word processor, sat on a desk near the foot of my bed. At night when I got up to go to the bathroom, the Pivot looked at me, hooded in the dark, but plugged in, ready to hum at the flick of a switch. In each studio hung a series of "tombstones," wooden markers inscribed by successive artists with names and dates of residence. It was not easy to lie on my bed, staring at the meadow outside my window, without being aware of those ghostly writers, their typewriters, their pages of prose and poetry, their eventual books. The air was heavy with purpose. So I couldn't think of the mud races without wondering how I could use them.

When Dan pulled into the fairgrounds, all I could see was dust. Hundreds of cars already lined the parking lots. The sun was hot, and as we walked through the long rows, kicking up more dust, I began to remember I didn't like crowds. At the gate we had to pay five dollars; this admitted us to a row of stalls selling T-shirts, woven plastic cowboy hats, embossed belts, and nylon hair bows studded with rhinestones. To the right was another gate to low bleachers edging a field where the mud races would be held. Although the races wouldn't begin for half an hour, the bleachers were already filling up. Nothing seemed to be happening on the field, so we decided to have dinner.

Following a stream of people past the cowboy hats and nylon bows, we soon found the food booths. Each sold one or two specialties: vegetable tempura; french fries and fried onion rings; fried pizza; deep-fried doughnuts. The quintessential booth simply advertised "Fried Dough." Walking between the booths, I could hear the constant sizzle of hot grease. Glenda, Mark, and Adrian disappeared into the beer tent, but Dan and I, hungry, forged on. Next to one stand we found a rickety card table with chairs, where, after forays to different booths, we assembled dinner. I ate two hot dogs, french fries, half an order of fried onion rings, two Diet Pepsis, a piece of fried dough with sugar and cinnamon, and a dairy dessert called Moo Lite.

I listed everything to myself with a kind of awe as I ate it. When I was young, I could have even drunk the fat this food had been fried in without ill effects. In recent years, however, my stomach has become a delicate seismograph, registering the decibels of cream sauce, pecan pie, and Vietnamese egg rolls. I keep a bottle of Gelusil in the bathroom cabinet.

But maybe, I encouraged myself, things might not happen here as they do at home. Perhaps the regular laws of daily life are suspended at the Cheshire County Fair, as they are at the MacDowell Colony. Besides, the hot dogs, onion rings, french fries, fried dough, and Moo Lite might be material. I could imagine an essay about returning to the pungent flavors of junk food after years of pasta, broiled swordfish, and cold chicken. But in just a few bites I sensed a serious problem: flavor. There wasn't any. Under its slathering of mustard the hot dog was depressingly bland, heavy breading buried the sharp taste of onions, and even the french-fried potatoes registered mainly as fried.

Fortunately, dinner was fun anyway. Dan and I ate, laughed, and watched passersby, men with duck-billed caps, potbellied men who clearly didn't jog or worry about it, hard-muscled men in Hawaiian shirts, dressed-up women holding tight to the men. Despite our disguises of jeans, work shirts, and sneakers, our little MacDowell group were clearly outsiders. But we blended enough into the crowd to head unnoticed to the bleachers for the mud races. This was it, I thought, settling into my seat and waiting for the action to begin. The real material.

Only the action didn't begin. I found myself staring at an untidy mound of loosely piled earth, sloped at each end into ramps leading to the packed dirt of the enclosure. The mound itself was perhaps a hundred feet long, with high sides and an interior trough. Two yellow Caterpillars were slowly creeping around the mound, shoving and hauling the dirt, though into what further shape I couldn't quite tell. Off at one side stood a fire truck with hoses, which had evidently watered the trough before we arrived. Maybe that was what had drawn the early crowds.

Back and forth the Cats ambled, their treads groaning, the mound sinking a little here, rising a little there. My stomach began rising and sinking a little too. I regretted the onion rings. Meanwhile an announcer explained over a loudspeaker what would happen when the course was finally ready. The drivers, I found, did not race together down the field. Instead, each took a separate turn, starting at one end of the mound and trying to drive through the trough of mud to the other end. The driver was judged on how far he or she went and the amount of time before the vehicle hopelessly bogged down. When momentum ceased, a mud-side referee dropped a red flag. After all the contestants had taken their turns, the one with the best time-and-distance score won.

In this first class, the announcer went on, speaking carefully but still losing me in technical phrases, everyone had to use D.O.T. (Department of Transportation) tires and meet certain other restrictions. In the second, "supermodified" class, they could upgrade their tires. In the third, "open" class, they could evidently transform their vehicles completely. I heard him say that there were eighteen entrants in the first class alone, and as I looked at the long line of four-wheeled machines stretching to the edge of the field, my heart sank. This was not going to be a speedy evening.

Half an hour after posted starting time, the first machine started its engine, roared into life, and rolled up the ramp. To pass the time, we had been picking favorites. I had chosen a red Jeep, which had the air of a David among Goliaths, loomed over by mammoth-wheeled pickups, giant-sized dune buggies, and a few vehicles that looked like truncated buses on stilts. Each was painted, sometimes lavishly decorated, and even named. Our MacDowell group, whose ages hovered on either side of forty, rather liked "Midlife Crisis" and "Grounds for Divorce."

When the first machine, a square blue open-sided truck, was at the top of the ramp, ready to head into the trough of mud, an official attached a long cable from its rear end to one of the big Caterpillars waiting on the field. When the truck got stuck, Dan explained, the Cat

82

would pull it out. After several false starts, involving axle adjustments, a snapped cable, and various consultations with referees, the driver fastened his helmet and revved up his engine. The noise was deafening, with a dominant strain of broken mufflers and an undertone of jackhammers attacking concrete.

As I plugged my ears, the referee dropped his flag and the truck lurched forward into the mud. Almost immediately, in two or three seconds, it ground to a halt, its motor whining in a new high key of frustrated rage, smoke pouring from its hood, a smell of burning fuels drifting into the crowd, and large brown droplets of mud raining on truck, driver, referee, and the closest bystanders. The first race was over. After a short delay, the blue truck was ignominiously hauled backward from the mud pile, its driver stoically staring straight ahead, and the next machine in line began to rev its engine.

The race, so to speak, continued. One after another, the four-wheeled rigs lumbered up the ramp while the announcer described their specifications, kind and size of engine, nitrous oxide power assists, and other modifications. A few got a foot or two farther or faster than the others, but no one seemed able to progress past a certain point, a mud barrier that everyone hit like a wall at about thirty feet. My favorite entry, the red Jeep, driven surprisingly by a young woman, took a fast flying start and plowed a bit farther than most. But she too drove into the wall of mud, spun her wheels, and stopped.

Half an hour into the race, at about the sixth entrant, I began to feel a little funny. When my stomach starts to churn, especially if I'm tired, I sometimes get flushed, my vision blurs a bit, and I get a shaky sensation in my knees. That was happening right now. I thought of my quiet studio, its screen doors open to the fading light on the pine-edged meadow, and my comfortable bed with its soothing white spread. I didn't know if I would last until the eighteenth mud race, let alone the remaining two classes. But I didn't want to spoil everyone else's good time and ask to go home.

Nor did I want to leave the group and stretch out, as I knew I easily could, in Dan's Mazda with its fold-down seats. One of my unexpected pleasures at MacDowell had been realizing that I could make an accepted place in a strange community, among men and women whose lives, careers, and personal geography were often radically different from mine. At home, I lived a somewhat insular life with my small, much-loved, and protective family. I was often afraid of what might happen if fate were to destroy that protection. Now I knew that if I ever again needed the skills and confidence to find new friends in unfamiliar territory, I had them.

So I stayed in the bleachers with Dan, Mark, Adrian, and Glenda, who were talking and telling jokes with contagious gaiety. While laughing, I was also silently counting the slow progress of each mud racer: nine, ten, eleven. Across the field I could see the lights of the midway brightening in the growing darkness, the twirling arms of an octopus ride, the stately curve of the Ferris wheel, the dip and whirl of twist-'em cars. The lights twinkled and blurred, my stomach whirled, and I tried to look somewhere on the horizon for material.

But all I saw in front of me was mud. Another vehicle tore into the muck, foundered briefly, spun its wheels, and died. There was something depressing about all this. I thought of the driver, who had spent so much time and money preparing his vehicle, equipping and decorating it, and then slamming his weeks and dollars of work into the mud. For what? For the chance to enter another, bigger mud race somewhere else? I began to take the names of "Grounds for Divorce" and "Midlife Crisis" more seriously. How dismal might someone's life be if this were how he chose to enliven it?

Then I began to wonder about the mud race as metaphor. I often felt like one of those drivers: taking a deep breath, revving my engine, and heading straight into an impenetrable and absolutely opaque wall of mud. At night at MacDowell, I sometimes lay awake and thought of two friends who had both died a few weeks before I arrived here. One had been my closest woman friend for fifteen years, just my age, and I could not yet reconcile myself to her long, excruciating death. When I agonized about where she was now, or about when or how I myself might die, my mind soon ran into a blank wall of mud.

This was not material I wanted to write about. So at intermission, while the supermodified class was changing its tires, I urged our group to head to the midway. Off we went, holding hands or elbows so we wouldn't lose each other, ideal fair-goers, cheerful, cooperative, and ready to be amused. On the route to the midway we passed the fair's one sideshow attraction, a covered flatbed truck advertising the "World's Largest Pig." Admission was only seventy-five cents. We looked at each other, reached for our change, and filed inside. Suddenly I found myself face to snout with an apparition that seemed as grotesque and unlikely as the mud races. Yet this pig was as real as the square blue truck with monster-sized wheels, as real as the mound of mud. It was lying asleep on a bed of straw, its sides heaving up and down with the effort of breathing. A posted clipping from *People* magazine said that the pig weighed more than a ton. I believed it. The pig was the size of a small cow, probably four feet from hoof to shoulder, a mountainous pig, a pig that defied ordinary laws of nature. But I didn't see this pig as a metaphor for anything. I left the enclosure quickly; it was just more pig than I wanted to think about.

I felt better when I was walking, though the rides, the crowds, and the flashing lights seemed even more blurred than they had from the bleachers. But despite my shakiness, I was no readier to leave the warmth of our companionable little group and go back to the car. I pictured myself lying on the seat, gazing into the dark, alone in an infinite parking lot of empty cars. So I sat instead on the steps of a carnival truck and watched the others persuade themselves into a dizzying ride whose flimsy seats turned upside down while circling wildly into the sky. As they whirled by, Glenda looking amazed and Mark frozen, I waved but stayed put. Thinking obsessively about death, I was not about to court it.

As we wandered among the stands, betting quarters on colored squares, pausing at dart games and ball tosses, marveling at the flamboyant ugliness of the large stuffed pandas, I relaxed. Soon we could go home. But I still didn't think I would have anything to write about.

After we had lost more quarters than we wanted to count, and won only one plastic whistle among us, Glenda and Adrian suggested we find the beer tent again. But Mark, whose poet's nerves were sensitive to unspoken feelings, spoke up: "I think Susan's tired," he said. "Why don't we go home? We can always have a drink at the Folkways after dropping her off." I smiled at him gratefully. Dan, who had missed the intermediate stages of the mud races without complaint, asked if we would mind catching the last few minutes before heading out. As we rounded the end of the midway, we could hear a familiar roar and whine.

We were in time only for the last two races. Now the drivers could use any equipment on their trucks, including scoops and paddle wheels. A contestant hurtled into the muck, and this time, to my amazement, hit the formerly impassable wall, staggered, slowed, but then gunned again, while the mud flew in sheets, and rammed his way through and down the opposite ramp. The crowd cheered. Now this, I thought, might have been worth watching. But it was almost over. The last contestant flipped over, wheels waving helplessly, the driver unhurt but defeated. We did not wait to hear an official announcement of whose time and distance had won.

In Dan's car on the way home, we talked about art, nightmares, jobs we'd had, New York and Minnesota, and what we had missed for dinner back at MacDowell. I thought about what an odd, funny, and friendly evening it had been. I was a thousand miles from home, with four people I'd never heard of two weeks ago, and we were talking as easily as if we'd known each other for years. On nights when I was afraid of being left alone, I could remind myself about tonight.

As the New Hampshire forests poured in and out of the van's headlights, Mark spoke of a year in Missouri he'd spent as a self-proclaimed landscaper, while his girlfriend drove an ice cream truck around a nearby army base. "That would be a great story," I said. I had been trying to convince him to try prose; I always worry about my friends who are poets. As I urged Mark to put some of his anecdotes down on paper, assuring him that readers like me are really curious about other lives, I realized I was also explaining why I write. I'm curious about my own life, just as I want to know about Mark's. What does it all mean? Some incidents nag and tease at my mind, like an unsolved mystery, until I try to interpret them. I need to make sense of my experience, to give shape to what otherwise is a chaos of feeling and memory. I write about what happens to me so that I can understand it.

As Philip Roth says, it's all material. But sometimes,

like the night at the mud races, I don't recognize the meaning in the material until I've finished writing about it. Even then, long after the mud has settled, I am seldom able to sum everything up in a single line. "Just remember," Dan said once during that long evening, noting my restless squirming, "mud racing is a subtle sport." He grinned ironically, but maybe he was right.

# Turning onto
# Less-Traveled Roads

"LET'S SPEND the last three days in London," my husband said, looking up from a table spread with well-worn tourist maps of Devon, Dorset, Somerset, and Cornwall. I thought for a moment, images rapidly clicking through my mind. I saw us strolling down Birdcage Walk on a sunny Sunday afternoon, admiring extravagant clumps of searing blue delphinium; sitting sedately in a black square taxi as it careened around Hyde Park Corner; panting down the escalators to catch the tube for a last-minute matinee at the Barbican. I heard the tapping of umbrellas along Knightsbridge, smelled the fresh sausage rolls in Justin de Blanck's, watched the slow brown sweep of the Thames under the Hungerford Footbridge. I examined delicate teacups in the Reject China Shop in Beauchamp Place and fingered the impossibly expensive cashmere sweaters in the Burlington Arcade. Then I reluctantly turned off my projector.

"No," I heard myself say. "This time I don't want to go to London. I'd rather spend those last three days in Mrs. Jackson's country inn near Bude, where we can drive to that beach that stretches out for miles." Not go to London on a trip to England? What was wrong with me?

I had similarly surprised myself on our last trip to

89

California, where twice a year in Mendocino we walk, watch for whales, and listen to the restless surf. To get there, we fly to San Francisco, rent a car, and drive north. San Francisco has always been my favorite American city, brimming with romantic memories of my graduate-school years, still dazzling my midwestern eyes with its pastel houses, tumbling hills, fog, ocean, and flower carts. But we no longer plan to stay one or two nights there; although I look longingly backward as we cross the Golden Gate Bridge, we keep going. If we only have a week, I want to spend every minute of it in our rented one-room cottage on the Mendocino headlands.

"When a man is tired of London, he is tired of life," Samuel Johnson pronounced with such incontrovertible authority that he has been quoted by Anglophiles for more than two hundred years. When I pointed on a tabletop map to a spot on the Cornish coast instead of the large black print of London, I thought I heard Johnson's accusing voice. Was I tired of life? That night, as I walked thoughtfully around my nearby city lake, I examined myself. What had happened to me as a traveler?

At twenty, on my first trip to London, I don't think I ever stayed in my room except to sleep. When I wasn't in summer-school classes, I was walking the city, eagerly unfolding my A-to-Z map at every intersection, its brightly colored notations promising marvels on every unexplored street. Later, in my thirties, I traveled by myself to London, staving off loneliness by touring museums, scouring shops, and attending plays and concerts every evening. I reveled then in the surge along Oxford Street, the after-theater bustle toward the Piccadilly underground, the discreet jostling of the dowdy but regal ladies in Harrods Food Hall. Eating a cold supper cross-legged on my hotel bed, I heard the endless surge of motors as evidence that life was whirling outside my windows, waiting for me.

But a few years ago, not long after I turned forty, I noticed I was beginning to feel differently about London. I was still eager when the Gatwick train pulled into Victoria, when I stopped at a corner pub for my first glass of sweet cider, when I opened the *Times* to the competing temptations of theater listings. But listening to traffic, I tossed uneasily at night. When I descended toward a crowded underground station, I fought claustrophobia. I had to struggle with jet lag for several days before I stopped yawning during the second act of a play.

On this visit to London, as always, I couldn't shut out the siren song of a great city. Here I am, London whispered irresistibly: you haven't much time, you've spent a lot of money to get here, see what you can before it's too late. Though I often longed to nap those first afternoons, I couldn't bear to pass up the new landscape show at the V and A, or the Blakes at the Tate, or the silk scarves at Liberty's. So I'd tie my newly sensible shoes and set out.

The truth came to me a week later — it seldom arrives on time — when I stood on top of a hill in the middle of Exmoor, overlooking other sun-dappled hills. My husband and I had left London, reluctantly at first, for a quiet inn deep in the West Country. No, I realized, as the wind blew over the moor, brushing me lightly on its way to unseen slopes beyond the horizon, I wasn't tired of life. I was just tired.

At this time of my life what I needed was far different from the yearnings of my eager, untried twenty-year-old self. I no longer craved the same kind of restless adventure, searching out ever-new places and people, seeing what I'd read about to find out if it were true. Then I wanted to fill in gaps on my own personal map, which was as big and white and blank as the enticingly unexplored Congo that seduces Marlow in Conrad's *Heart of Darkness.* Now my map has layers scribbled all over it; it is a palimpsest I often have trouble reading. I need to sort out the notations, discover where the truly important places lie, and learn the best routes to return to them. My adventures at the moment are inner ones.

When I am deciphering and pondering these complicated scribblings, I need to concentrate. Behind me I leave days filled with telephone calls, lunchtime conversations, students' questions, my daughter's insistent voice, taped music and television, computer clicks, bells and buzzers and hums. Why should I trade this noise for the different but even higher decibels of a city?

At this time in my life, I want to walk, think, and dream. I long for wide vistas of sea or sky or moorland so I can feel my mind stretch out. I search for gentle hills or riverside paths or forest walks to ease my body out of tautness and tension. I like fresh winds to blow debris and dust out of my stacked and jumbled memories. And though I'm happy with a chosen companion, I don't want anyone else nudging me or looking over my shoulder. Who can unfold and study a personal chart in the midst of a crowd?

So I send for brochures from English country-house inns, consider Norwegian coastal steamers, think about renting a farmhouse in northern Italy, remember the off-season calm of a seaside village in southern Crete. Someday I'll probably be ready again for the exciting hum of a city at dusk as restaurants gleam and taxis hurry, the rustle of programs as the curtain lifts, and the jeweled enclosures of museums. But right now, I plan to look for hidden turnoffs on less-traveled roads. There, at a spot where I see more fields than houses, perhaps on a river bluff or at the edge of a meadow or on a dune looking out to sea, I can sit quietly for a while. Perhaps then I'll know where I really want to travel next.

# In Search of Quiet Places

TWENTY COLLEGE STUDENTS crowded around the small log church, carefully touching its rough-hewn sides, trying the lock on the front door and then, frustrated, briefly pressing their noses to some of its narrow dusty windows. I was amused by the picture they made: in eighteen years of teaching, I had never seen twenty-year-olds anxious to get into a church. They were not particularly drawn by religion; for them, the little church was simply a curiosity, a historic monument in a section of St. Paul they were exploring on a field trip. But as I stood behind these politely jostling students, I must have been more startled by the picture than I realized. For days afterward, I thought about it.

What does a locked church signify? What possibilities does it foreclose? Why did I have such a poignant sense of loss when I saw young people tugging at that door? What might they have found if they'd gotten in? Perhaps I was registering an awareness that my students' lives, like mine, are often packed and pressured, ready to explode. Is a church somewhere to cool down, stop sizzling, return to normal? Is it a place to find peace and quiet, two qualities so tied to each other that the very phrase has become a cliché? Where can they go to be alone with their thoughts? Surely not in today's dormitories, where student freedoms often result in an anarchy of noise. Where does *anyone* in an urban environment go to be alone with his or her thoughts? I began wondering about quiet places.

I know that most churches in the Twin Cities are locked. Indeed, when I arrived not long ago at one downtown for a meeting, I had to buzz at the door, as if I were entering a security-conscious jewelry store, and identify myself to a faceless speaker before I was let inside. My own Summit Avenue congregation securely fastens its portals against intruders, and when once I stopped biking, on impulse, at a modest but appealing church in a humbler neighborhood, I found it shut tight too. I don't blame anyone. I understand all too well the fears of burglary, vandalism, and abuse that make us all lock our offices, cars, and houses.

But I dimly remember in the small town of my childhood how, on my way home from school or from a friend's house, I sometimes wandered into the shady coolness of the church my family attended. It was always open. Not a very devout child, I didn't go in to pray or do anything in particular. I just walked softly into the sanctuary, where I paused in the almost palpable stillness, so different from the rustling hush of Sundays, and listened to the silence so intently I thought I might hear the dust motes moving in the mellow half-light that filtered through the yellow-tinted windows. Sometimes I even sat in a pew for a few tentative minutes, enjoying being all by myself under the soaring oak arches.

The other quiet place in town was our public library, which always seemed to be deserted, and where the silence was rigidly enforced by formidable librarians. It was not large — three main rooms, a mezzanine, and a storage basement — but somehow I could always find a corner where I felt completely alone. All that disturbed my peace was a rare whisper, the occasional crackle of a turning page, or the heavy thunk of an encyclopedia returning to rest.

Someone looking for a quiet place in the Twin Cities — preferably indoors, since bad weather makes lakeshore and park bench uncomfortable spots to meditate — would have a hard time. Although libraries are more accessible than churches, many are not as peaceful as they once were. Urged to offer information retrieval, duplicating services, microfilms, tapes, and various community programs, they often hum with electronics and bustle with activity. Their tables and chairs are distractingly crowded, and their hidden corners are difficult to find.

Where, then, can someone in the Twin Cities go for silence? I am fortunate to have my own study, yet I sometimes wish to escape from its surrounding distractions: doorbell, telephone, a desk piled with bills and unanswered letters, and reminders everywhere in the house of waiting responsibilities, from heaped laundry baskets to dried-out plants. Some of my students tell me they can't study well in their rooms for the same reasons. One admitted he used to climb high on the outside fire escape of a nearby old building, where he was often cold but satisfactorily alone; now that the building has been demolished, he doesn't know where else to go. He wishes he knew of a nearby café, open at all hours, that offered the same kind of daily refuge Hemingway describes in his famous story "A Clean Well-Lighted Place." But no sensible owner of a restaurant or bar today encourages its clientele to hang around with little money to spend.

Someone desperate for silence can be very ingenious. When her child was young, one mother I know used to shut herself in the shower stall, with the bathroom door locked, until the hot water gave out, because as long as the water beat a steady tattoo on the tiles, she couldn't hear anything else. A teaching colleague of mine drives the long way to work, meandering miles on off-freeway roads, because he says that is the only time and place — early morning and late afternoon in his car — that he is able to be alone to think.

Perhaps quiet places are rare because too few of us admit how much we need them. Noise seems to be the norm, and we are afraid to demand equal time for silence. On a sunny fall day when I walk across my college campus and hear rock music blaring from open windows, assaulting other students who are stretched out below on the lawn, I am always amazed that someone trying to rest or read doesn't march upstairs in anger. I wonder why student protesters, fierce to demonstrate for other kinds of rights, don't hurl intrusive stereos out the window. Along our lakes, boom boxes invade personal space with the pertinacity of giant shrieking mosquitoes. Like everyone else, I am too timid to ask to have the dials turned down.

Perhaps it is too hard to explain *why* we need silence. I often say apologetically to a smoker who is starting to light up at a dinner table or in a committee meeting, "Do you mind not smoking? I'm allergic." That's sort of true, since cigarette smoke gives me headaches. But I haven't learned how to say to someone making noise, "Do you mind?" The standard excuse would be "I need to think," but I don't often use it. I'm afraid it sounds pretentious, as if I were on the verge of some important intellectual discovery, about to revise the theory of relativity or definitely solve the problem of evil.

Besides, I don't need quiet so I can think, exactly — at least in the sense of coherent, organized thought. I need quiet so I can clear my mind for thinking. Since my life is filled with so many jumbled impressions, glimpses of other people, bulletins from other places, recalled conversations, problems proposed for solution,

97

provoking puzzles, troubling or tantalizing ideas, and just plain static, I often have to retreat to silence to sort it all out. I need to file everything away so I can sense some blank spaces again. I accumulate mental clutter like an under-the-eaves attic, which can be, when ordered and swept, a soothingly quiet place, somewhere to hide from the family downstairs, offering a chance to go through boxes of old memories.

I don't remember feeling so strongly about quiet when I was younger. Excitement then always meant lots of noise: parades, cheering sections at high-school games, Elvis Presley full blast at after-game dances, the roar and whine of the midway at the state fair, and, a few years later, the bustle of big-city streets, blared announcements and milling crowds at airports, laughter and clinking and music at holiday parties. My own fifteen-year-old never seems to need quiet, which she finds *"boring,"* a state from which cassette player, telephone, and television rescue her during most waking hours. If she knew more quiet places in her daily environment, would she seek them out? I'm not sure.

Around the age of forty, I began to notice how much I craved time to myself, and how I wanted to spend that time in quiet places. I am no longer resilient when floods of noise wash over me; in fact, I frequently find myself flattened. Never having learned how to shut out the world, maybe I now listen even more acutely to meanings and intonations, trying to understand them. Perhaps my mental attic is simply stuffed with too many bags and boxes, and I can't make space for new accumulations as easily. Certainly, like many people in midlife, I find myself starting to ask questions that I never before found particularly compelling, questions about where I am going, what I am doing, and why. Those kinds of questions need plenty of silence to move around in.

So I think about quiet places. A friend of mine, trying to help, recently lent me a tape of self-guided imagery, which instructs me to imagine a peaceful spot and travel there. Stretching with pleasure, I can easily picture my favorites: a surf-pounded beach north of Mendocino, a wooded bluff at Lake Pepin, or a windy lakeshore in northern Wisconsin. So I know I can create a quiet place in my mind. But I still need a real one in my daily life. I think most people do.

I wish we had more outposts, not of progress, but of silence. I wish I could see a tourist map of the Twin Cities, the kind with funny little symbols for historic sites, campgrounds, and public beaches, that was instead covered with plain dots — no towers, arches, or anything intimidating — that symbolized quiet places. Maybe it wouldn't attract a new horde of visitors, but it would offer possibilities for voyagers embarked on inner exploration. I wouldn't mind a license plate that proudly proclaimed Minnesota the state of ten thousand quiet places. We might be surprised how many people would seek them out.

# FOUR

# On Picking Raspberries

# On Picking Raspberries

AS I LOOKED DOWN the rows of green bushes, brown edges curling in the sun, I didn't see many raspberries. A few red dots here and there, some pale, half-ripe berries hanging from the top branches. I wondered again what I was doing here. Earlier this morning, as I was racing through breakfast, dishes, and bed making so I could get here before they closed the fields at 9 A.M., I knew that this trip might seem foolish. Half an hour's worth of gas each way, three hours of baby-sitting, two hours of hard, hot work in the fields, all for ten or twelve pints of raspberries that I could buy prepicked, washed, and packed in the grocery store for two dollars a pint. I knew it didn't make economic sense.

I walked past the first few bushes in my assigned row, picking the berries I could see easily. There weren't many. I would have to bend down, turn aside the prickly branches, search under the leaves for the hidden clusters the birds and earlier pickers might have missed. Glancing regretfully at my freshly laundered jeans, I plopped onto the muddy ground, my knees sinking deep into the dirt. Then I began prowling through the shady green tangle in front of my nose. Almost immediately I found a handful of huge ripe berries, so juicy that they fell off the branch at my touch, and I popped them into my mouth. Now I was hooked, and I knew I would stay in this hot field until the sun burned my face and hands, the mosquitoes raised welts under my shirt, and my ten pint baskets were full to the brim.

Why do I do it? Why, every year in July, do I search for notices in the newspapers about the raspberry fields? I'm no country girl; I've lived for years quite happily in the heart of St. Paul, a fair-sized city. But picking raspberries has become one of my arts of survival.

I discovered it in desperation one summer morning some years ago. I was waiting for a man I loved, something I'm not very good at, despite a lot of practice. He had called to tell me he was home from California, that he was coming to see me in four hours, and I knew from the tone of his voice that he was also going to say goodbye again. I didn't know how to pass the time until noon. Of my two best friends, one was at work and the other at a golf lesson, and the walls of my house pressed in upon me, seeming to close off all my possibilities. I had to get out, to keep very busy, and I also had to figure out what to serve for lunch. I thought of the expensive raspberries, cushioned like jewels in a box, that I had resolutely passed by the day before in Lund's, and of someone who once had mentioned a pick-your-own place not far from St. Paul. A glance at "Home Produce" in the want ads, and I grabbed my map and set out.

Driving along the uncrowded freeway in the early morning forced my mind to leave home as well. As I whizzed past the giant car lots, hulking cement restaurants, and sprawling shopping centers and warehouses, I could sense all the activity beginning to whir into motion this hot summer day. I continued on, past Montgomery Ward, where I could stop on the way back to get my daughter a sleeping bag; past the turnoff to Lyndale Garden Center, where I wanted to buy a few perennials to stick in the bare spaces of my garden; past

Highway 100, which would lead me to a cousin I hadn't seen for far too long. Places to go, things to do, afterward.

Turning off the freeway, turning again onto another route, I suddenly found myself in real country. Scattered houses set far back from the road, bits of a startlingly blue lake behind trees, farms buried beyond fields of corn, boards tacked to trees announcing "Honey for Sale" and "Fresh Eggs," only a few cars on the dusty road ahead of me. I began to breathe more deeply and quietly, glancing from side to side at the wide green spaces that were already sending up waves of heat. Though I was on a strange route, I felt I knew exactly where I was, in the middle of a state whose familiar summer stretched out for hundreds of miles in any direction.

When I followed the scrawled "U-Pick" signs down a winding side road to one of those hidden farms, I found I wasn't the only one who wanted to pick berries that morning. I had to stand in line to get my baskets weighed before I started, behind a woman tugging two restless children, another woman with her blond hair in curlers, and still another, efficiently clad in swimsuit and sun hat, all chatting companionably about the weather, the price of raspberries, and the mosquitoes. My impending melodrama seemed very far away.

As I picked and picked down the rows that morning, I could feel the climbing sun beating fiercely through my thin shirt. Sweat poured down my back; an occasional breeze ruffled my damp hair; sometimes I had to stop and wipe the perspiration from my face on my sleeve so I could see what I was doing. I thought of nothing but the heat, the dirt, how thirsty I was, the number of baskets I had left to fill, and how many raspberries might be buried inside the next bush. When I found several handfuls on one branch, I was filled with

105

delight, as though I had uncovered a small treasure. I remembered how the heroine of one of my favorite books served wild raspberries with bread and butter to an important visitor on a festive occasion. Serving these berries to someone I loved would be a special offering too.

Baskets at last filled, piled high with berries so ripe they oozed juice through the bottom slats, I rose from my cramped position and stretched. My jeans felt like wet leather plastered to my legs, my shirt clung, my eyebrows dripped. The sun overhead blinded me when I tried to clean my dark glasses. I smelled hot and dirty, I was covered with bites, and my hands were badly scratched. But I knew I would soon be home, in a cool, darkened house, and I could shower for at least half an hour before my guest arrived. I could put on a clean, light dress and feel much better. I was glad to remember how easily some things can be washed away.

That afternoon after he left — he didn't stay long, wasn't very hungry, managed only one bowlful of berries — I labored in the kitchen, crying, blowing my nose, but mechanically washing, sugaring, packing my raspberries for the freezer in neat little white boxes. Down in the basement, stacked in cold darkness, they would wait until some bleak January day when I could bring them up into the sunshine, cover them with milk, and think back to summer. I would be able to remember this day — the hot, sweaty morning; the short, bitter lunch; the numbing afternoon — and all of it would be part of a past I would then taste only as slightly sour raspberries.

So this summer I pick raspberries as a reminder of the ways we all find to survive pain and loss. I pick them too because I love their dark winy taste, the slight crunch of seeds in my mouth, and the dots of color they make on bowls of crisp cereal and over vanilla ice cream. I also pick them because, having grown up in Iowa, I know the value of a dollar, and I can gorge myself on berries only when I know they didn't cost me two dollars a pint. My motives may be mixed, but my raspberries aren't. I keep them pure and simple, never stirring them into a soufflé, muddling them in a crust, or dissolving them into jelly. I roll them in my mouth, and I take my time when I eat them.

# Going to the Movies

I.

AARON TAKES ME only to art films. That's
what I call them, anyway: strange movies with vague
poetic images I don't always understand, long dreamy
movies about a distant Technicolor past, even longer
black-and-white movies about the general meaningless-
ness of life. We do not go unless at least one reputable
critic has found the cinematography superb. We went
to *The Devil's Eye*, and Aaron turned to me in the middle
and said, "My God, this is *funny*." I do not think he was
pleased.

When Aaron and I go to the movies, we drive our
cars separately and meet by the box office. Inside the
theater he sits tentatively in his seat, ready to move if
he can't see well, poised to leave if the film is disappointing. He leans away from me, careful not to touch
the bare flesh of his arm against the bare flesh of mine.
Sometimes he leans so far I am afraid he may be touching the woman on his other side instead. If the movie
is very good, he leans forward too, peering between the
heads of the couple in front of us. The light from the
screen bounces off his glasses; he gleams with intensity,
sitting there on the edge of his seat, watching the screen.
Once I tapped him on the arm so I could whisper a
comment in his ear. He jumped.

After *Belle de Jour* Aaron said he wanted to ask me if he could stay overnight. "But I can't," he shook his head mournfully before I had a chance to answer, "because I know I never sleep well in strange beds." Then he apologized for asking. "It's just that after a film like that," he said, "I feel the need to assert myself."

II.

Bob takes me only to movies that he thinks have a redeeming social conscience. He doesn't call them films. They tend to be about poverty, war, injustice, political corruption, struggling unions in the 1930s, and the military-industrial complex. Bob doesn't like propaganda movies, though, and he doesn't like to be too depressed, either. We stayed away from *The Sorrow and the Pity*; it would be, he said, just too much. Besides, he assured me, things are never that hopeless. So most of the movies we see are made in Hollywood. Because they are always very topical, these movies offer what Bob calls "food for thought." When we saw *Coming Home,* Bob's jaw set so firmly with the first half hour that I knew we would end up at Poppin' Fresh Pies afterward.

When Bob and I go to the movies, we take turns driving so no one owes anyone else anything. We park far away from the theater so we don't have to pay for a space. If it's raining or snowing, Bob offers to let me off at the door, but I can tell he'll feel better if I go with him while he parks, so we share the walk too. Inside the theater Bob will hold my hand when I get scared if I ask him. He puts my hand firmly on his knee and covers it completely with his own hand. His knee never twitches. After a while, when the scary part is past, he loosens his hand slightly and I know that is a signal to take mine away. He sits companionably close, letting his jacket just touch my sweater, but he does not infringe. He thinks I ought to know he is there if I need him.

One night after *The China Syndrome* I asked Bob if he wouldn't like to stay for a second drink, even though it was past midnight. He thought awhile about that, considering my offer from all possible angles, but finally he said no. Relationships today, he said, have a tendency to move too quickly.

III.

Sam likes movies that are entertaining. By that he means movies that Will Jones in the *Minneapolis Tribune* loved and either *Time* or *Newsweek* rather liked; also movies that do not have sappy love stories, are not musicals, do not have subtitles, and will not force him to think. He does not go to movies to think. He liked *California Suite* and *The Seduction of Joe Tynan*, though the plots, he said, could have been zippier. He saw it all coming too far in advance, and that took the fun out. He doesn't like to know what is going to happen. "I just want my brain to be tickled," he says. It is very hard for me to pick out movies for Sam.

When Sam takes me to the movies, he pays for everything. He thinks that's what a man ought to do. But I buy my own popcorn, because he doesn't approve of it; the grease might smear his flannel slacks. Inside the theater, Sam makes himself comfortable. He takes off his jacket, puts one arm around me, and all during the movie he plays with my hand, stroking my palm, beating a small tattoo on my wrist. Although he watches the movie intently, his body operates on instinct. Once I inclined my head and kissed him lightly just behind his ear. He beat a faster tattoo on my wrist, quick and musical, but he didn't look away from the screen.

When Sam takes me home from the movies, he stands outside my door and kisses me long and hard. He would like to come in, he says regretfully, but his steady girlfriend in Duluth wouldn't like it. When the *Tribune* gives a movie four stars, he has to save it to see with her. Otherwise her feelings might be hurt.

IV.

I go to some movies by myself. On rainy Sunday afternoons I often sneak into a revival house or a college auditorium for old Technicolor musicals, *Kiss Me Kate, Seven Brides for Seven Brothers, Calamity Jane,* even, once, *The Sound of Music.* Wearing saggy jeans so I can prop my feet on the seat in front, I sit toward the rear where no one will see me. I eat large handfuls of popcorn with double butter. Once the movie starts, I feel completely at home. Howard Keel and I are old friends; I grin back at him on the screen, admiring all his teeth. I know the sound tracks by heart. Sometimes when I get really carried away I hum along with Kathryn Grayson, remembering how I once thought I would fill out a formal like that. Skirts whirl, feet tap, acrobatic young men perform impossible feats, and then the camera dissolves into a dream sequence I know I can comfortably follow. It is not, thank God, Bergman.

If I can't find an old musical, I settle for Hepburn and Tracy, vintage Grant or Gable, on adventurous days Claudette Colbert or James Stewart. Before I buy my ticket I make sure it will all end happily. If necessary, I ask the girl at the box office. I have never seen *Stella Dallas* or *Intermezzo*. Over the years I have developed other peccadilloes: I will, for example, see anything that is redeemed by Thelma Ritter. At the end of *Daddy Long Legs* I wait happily for the scene when Fred Clark, no longer angry, at last pours Thelma a convivial drink. They smile at each other, I smile at them, I feel they are smiling at me. In the movies I go to by myself, the men and women always like each other.

# In Praise
# of Minnesota Weather

IN PRAISE of *what?* Depending on what day in April a Minnesotan reads this, he or she might write a letter of protest. Icy sleet may be falling, forcing the cancellation of a shopping trip or a lunch date. Unseasonable snow may be wilting tender lettuce in the vegetable garden or breaking stems of tulips that had ventured into last week's sunshine. Or equally unseasonable heat may have left everyone breathless and uncomfortable, wondering about putting in the window air conditioner, while the tulips open, fade, and quickly die. The newspaper may have just trumpeted a new record: highs, lows, dry soil or flooding rivers, delayed budding or early thaw, late frost or the early breakup of ice. *Something* unusual is undoubtedly happening with the weather.

That is one of the reasons I have grown to like Minnesota weather: its unpredictability. Our weather gives me all kinds of excuses to change my plans without sounding frivolous. No, I tell my dentist in December, I can't come in today; it's not that I'm afraid to have two teeth filled, but I can't get my car out of the garage because the plows haven't come yet. Yes, I tell my husband in July, I think we should both quit work early and go for a swim to cool off. Weather helps me be reclusive, too. In January, I always keep my social engagements to a minimum, knowing that with my dread of driving in bad weather, I'd better not commit myself. Things may happen: blizzards, freezing rain, subzero temperatures that stall my car. So January is a good month to stay home and work, hibernating in my study like a sleepy bear, growling at intruders, sleeping late on dark mornings, and taking naps on snowy afternoons.

When I lived for a few years in Berkeley, California, an ideal climate for someone who likes coolish sunny days, the weather didn't prevent me from going anywhere. I couldn't change my mind about anything. On the other hand, such predictability wreaked havoc with my academic life. When I first arrived in Berkeley as a graduate student, I would get up in the morning, walk outside into the brilliant sun and cool breezes, and promptly decide that I couldn't possibly work on such a wonderful day. In Minnesota, those rare days, appearing occasionally in May, June, September, or October, are practically state holidays. A parade marches around the lakes, people pop up in parks like dandelions, a steady stream surges along the banks of the Mississippi. When sun and breezes come out, so do we. But for a graduate student, this attitude was almost fatal.

The unpredictability of Minnesota weather also gives us plenty to talk about. When I want to say something pleasant to the cheerful man who runs the hardware store, or I meet unexpectedly a critic who doesn't like my work, or I am seated during a long dinner next to a scholar whose book I haven't read, I am never at a loss for words. "And what do you think of the weather we're having?" will carry us nicely. We Minnesotans have even developed a shorthand exchange, something like code for "How-are-you, I'm-fine-thank-you, how-are-the-wife-and-kids, sorry-I-have-to-dash." The exchange goes something like this:

"Wow! Some weather we're having today!"

"Yeah, isn't it something?"

"It sure is awfully (cold, hot, wet, dry) for this time of year, don'tcha think?"

"Yeah, I hear we're in for a spell of it."

"Yeah. Hard to believe it's (January, February, March, April, May, June, July, August, September, October, November, December)."

"Well, I guess it's good for the (ducks, flowers, farmers, snowmobilers, Aquatennial, Winter Carnival)."

"Yeah, and you know what they say, if you don't like our weather, wait an hour and it'll change." Shared laughter. Commiserating shrugs. A bond of community strengthened once more.

Listening to such exchanges, I also hear finer shades of feeling that seem to me expressive of our Great Northern character. We not only tend to fatalism, tempered by cautious optimism (see above), but to a strong sense of guilt. Our sins, we're sure, will be dealt with firmly by the omnipotent and just weather gods. An assortment of people — a professor of philosophy as well as a gas station attendant — have said to me, "Great weather we're having." Pause. "But we'll pay for it, won't we?"

Although our day-to-day weather is unpredictable, we do know we'll have different seasons. Trees change color, snow falls, ice covers the lakes, then the ice melts, trees bud and turn green, the corn and tomatoes eventually grow and ripen, and the leaves start to turn again. I love the intense sensuousness of this changing scenery: the dazzling white sunlight on new snow, the rustle of brown leaves underfoot, the thunder and hard drumming of rain on the roof, the rich rank smell of my garden when hot sun follows a heavy rain.

I also welcome the reassurance of a recurring cycle; if I lived where the weather never changed, I think I might miss the sense of renewal I feel in spring and fall. Each season has its kind of psychic gift. When I wake to the first deep snowfall of winter, I look out on the hushed and covered world with an inner sense of peace. When the summer heat bakes me down to my toes, I slow down, forced to a languorous pace usually foreign to hard-driven Minnesotans.

And what would happen in a boring climate to my pleasure in dressing up? Of changing costumes like an actress in different scenes? I like to shed my bulky, knobbly sweaters in the spring and float through summer in a whoosh of cotton. In the fall, I unpack colored tights, mohair scarves, furry hats. I enjoy the different textures and weights of my seasonal coverings. I don't even mind being buried in a cocoon of down, light and warm, as long as I know I don't have to wear it forever.

Of course I know I am lucky: I can afford to enjoy Minnesota weather. I can buy a snug parka, pay my heating bills, turn on an air conditioner in summer. I am sure I would not sing praises of the winter if I had a sick child in a cold apartment, or of the summer if I had severe hay fever. I do not have to cope with a wheelchair or the fragility of aged and brittle bones. Those of us who *can* enjoy Minnesota's climate obviously have a special obligation to do what we can for those who find it a physical trial. I sympathize with the bitter woman who once told me, "They should have made Minnesota a national park. Then nobody would live here. People could just visit if they wanted to."

But speaking for myself, I do not want to move to Florida. I do not envy my friends who live all year in Tucson. I don't *think* I would want to return forever to northern California, though I'm not sure I'd want to be too strongly tempted. On most Minnesota days, I like to think I've come to agreeable terms. I've not only made my peace with winter but learned to turn the other cheek to be tanned in summer. I relish spring and fall, especially when, as Minnesotans say, they happen to come on a weekend. And I'm working on believing that when a good spell of weather comes, I *won't* have to pay for it later.

In fact, maybe writing this piece will placate the weather gods: a hymn of praise ought to be worth five straight days of sunshine in March, a week in the seventies in June, no frost until November, or one of those rare April days full of promise, brisk and clear with a hint of warmth, sunshine nudging the crocuses, snow almost melted, and the grass turning green. If today is like that, I'd like to think I did my part.

# Giggles

I LIKE the summer sounds of Lake Harriet: the quacks of jostling ducks, the splash of a glinting fish, crashing waves on a windy day. Aside from the irritating screech of tires and the blare of boxed music, I even enjoy human noises: trumpets echoing beyond the bandstand, an enticing tinkle from the ice cream cart, the friendly greetings of walkers. I especially like the sound of laughter, rising high in the light air after being muffled under heavy scarves all winter. One recent summer afternoon, I stopped to watch three small children on the beach. They were running in and out of the water, splashing and giggling, their delighted shrieks like those of excited birds. Later I passed two teenage girls, heads pressed close and shoulders touching, giggling so hard that they wobbled off the path.

As I walked home, I began thinking about giggles. I had been writing that day about my grandmother Lena, a Norwegian farmer's daughter from western Minnesota, who died before I was born. Though I have been trying to learn about Lena for some time, I haven't gotten very far. Her children tell me she was a good woman, loving, a careful mother, anxious that her children do well. But idiosyncrasies? Flaws? Dreams or disappointments? No one can remember. The only detail that has brought Grandmother alive for me so far is the fact that she giggled.

I heard this from Cousin Agnes, an aged niece of Lena's, who happily remembered a visit my grandmother had paid her mother. "Those sisters were so close," Cousin Agnes told me. "How excited Momma was when Aunt Lena came to stay! They were both older women then, with grown children, but they'd sit on Momma's bed and gossip and giggle for hours. I can still hear them. My, how they'd laugh!"

To know my grandmother giggled was a great gift. What little I understand of her — ill much of the time, married to an autocratic and hot-tempered man — is not cheering. I like to think of Lena and her sister, escaping from the heavy responsibilities of their large families, the planning and cleaning and cooking, and huddling for a while together on the soft bed, bunching pillows and digging their toes into the quilts as if they were children again. I try to hear them too, ripples of laughter behind the closed door, sharing private jokes and being — well, just a little silly.

Silliness and giggles are not much encouraged in our adult lives. They are so easily silenced by heavier, serious voices. I hear those voices everywhere in the public world. Health authorities exhort us to eat well, keep fit, stop smoking, and watch for the warning signs of cancer. Psychologists urge us to positive thinking, clear communication, self-assertiveness, personal autonomy, and so many other stern commandments that mental health seems as easy as carrying Moses' tablets around on our shoulders. Historians and sociologists alert us to the cliff edge beyond our next steps. Indeed, one glance at the morning newspaper will banish any effervescent silliness that might have started to bubble, wrinkling your nose or tingling in your toes, before it has a chance to rise to the surface. You put the paper down, solemnly, thinking of the state of the world — Star Wars, AIDS, pollution, starvation, torture, child abuse, rape — and no longer pay much attention to the Siamese trying to attack your feet under the blanket, crouching and pouncing in great dramatic leaps if you give the slightest provocative twitch.

We distrust giggles, calling them "infectious" or "a fit" as if they might be a health hazard. If moderately lucky, we do find humor in our lives. We laugh ironically — afterward — at the tricks life plays on us daily: the name forgotten just as a critical introduction is about to take place, the chocolates that arrive on the first day of a new diet, a tire gone flat en route to the airport. We laugh on cue at sitcoms and stand-up comics and movies that we permit to seize our funny bones and work them vigorously up and down. We half groan, ashamed of our response, at sick jokes. We grin, ho-ho, rumble, and occasionally belly-laugh.

But we do not often giggle. To giggle, my *Webster's* says without a trace of a smile, is "to laugh in a silly or undignified way." When I try to picture a truly dignified laugh, I begin to titter a bit myself. My own definition might be "to acknowledge with uncontrollable laughter the wonderful foolishness of human pretension," or, less ponderously, "to laugh like a child." Not long ago, looking at my high-school yearbook, I found an old picture of a friend I'd recently seen after more than twenty years. At lunch Marcie, now a lawyer, and I talked about our marriages, children, jobs, and the town and people we'd known as children. It was good talk, earnest and informative. But in the informal snapshot, taken at a slumber party, is another Marcie, dressed in pajamas with her hair in curlers and scrunched on a sofa with two other girls. All three of their faces are contorted with laughter, their mouths curving up toward their ears, their eyes almost closed. They are unaware of anything but their convulsions of hilarity, the joke they share, the fun they're having.

Behind my teenager's door, I can sometimes hear sounds like that, foolish, free, and unquenchable. I listen enviously to the note of total irresponsibility in those cackling, gleeful voices. When do those sounds change? When does laughter become more rooted, more tied to daily life, to sensible things? When do we stop acknowledging the possibility of a gaiety in life so profound that it can seize us and render us helpless, shaking, childish with laughter?

I hope my daughter will always have a girlfriend who can laugh with her the way she does now. I treasure the women whom I can call with some ludicrous tidbit, announcing breathlessly, "Guess what just happened?" and knowing when I've finished I'll hear a responsive snort or an explosion of snickers that will link my friend and me once more in a shared understanding of the lunacy of life. If she's lucky, as I am, she can share that kind of laughter with her husband too, though most men don't seem to giggle very often. Perhaps they are too worried about appearing responsible, in charge, and totally grown up. They miss a very important kind of bonding; when two people have seen in each other's eyes the same recognition of absurdity, they can trust each other more when they are serious. I wish President Reagan and Premier Gorbachev might sit together one day at a summit table, and then perhaps both simultaneously hearing, in an unexpected quiet moment when everyone had suddenly stopped talking, a particularly pompous, self-important diplomat loudly break wind, catch each other's eye, and begin to giggle.

I'd feel a lot better about the possibilities for world peace.

So as I walk around the lake on a summer night, calming myself with the murmur of water and the soft whoosh of leaves, I also listen for the sound of giggles. They give me hope.

# FIVE

# Birthday Balloons

# Birthday Balloons

WHEN MY DAUGHTER asks plaintively, "Mommy, isn't it time to start planning my birthday party?" I get a funny feeling in my stomach, as though I've just eaten too much goocy white frosting. But I try to respond as a Good Mommy should. "Of course, dear," I say with a benevolent smile. "What kind of party would you like?"

"Oh, maybe roller skating at that big indoor rink at Lake Minnetonka and a movie and then dinner at our house with lots of games afterward," Jennie proposes casually.

I put my book down. This is serious business and will require my full attention. "Well, possibly *one* of those activities, if you don't invite too many guests, but I can only get four into our car and I don't know any of the other girls' parents well enough to ask them to drive, and besides, it may snow, and no, I don't think dinner is a good idea, unless you've suddenly started liking hot dogs. What kind of games?" I try to divert our energies into a manageable channel.

"A treasure hunt," Jennie says with definiteness. Now she too is serious. "I'll hide prizes and leave clues in funny places, like inside the refrigerator and litter box and piano and dresser." I picture half a dozen frantic nine-year-olds emptying the ice-cube tray, spilling the

125

soup, and rummaging through my panty hose. I try not to think of the litter box.

"Well . . . ," I say doubtfully, working toward a tactful no. Jennie interrupts. "Then a three-legged race would be fun, and could we have an egg toss?"

"In the *living room?*" I bleat, losing control. There is a pained silence. "How about a nice game of Sorry, and the rest of you could play Chinese checkers?"

"Muh-*ther*," says Jennie, with a mixture of anger and grief. "Are you *kidding?*" We look at each other for a few moments, while she accurately reads the expression on my face. "Mother," she asks with an uncanny thrust, "why don't you like birthday parties?"

"But I *do!*" I cry, wounded. At least, I like the *idea* of birthday parties. I do want Jennie to celebrate her special day, and I do want to mark appropriately another milestone in her headlong rush to womanhood. Has it really been ten years since I lay, tired but triumphant, in a cold hospital room, dazedly thinking of that small creature with tiny pursed lips who had just been carried into the nursery? How could time have passed so quickly? Can I make it slow down for a moment if I pause at birthdays?

But Jennie is also right. I *don't* really like birthday parties. Not only do they make me wince with the hours of planning, preparation, and shopping ahead, but they trouble me in other ways. They raise delicate social issues. Who should be invited? Who will be left out? What about the daughter of the other woman in the car pool, or the next-door neighbor, or the lonely child who phones night after night? And how about the whole business of presents? At most parties they seem more like required tickets, collected at the door, than tokens of affection. As a young birthday child rips off careful wrappings, while guests sigh with envy or loudly worry about their own offerings, I feel uncomfortable.

Mostly what I don't like about birthday parties, though, are my own memories. I always wanted my birthday to be wonderful. My mother did her best, baking delicious homemade cakes, and diligently searching for the requested present, but somehow I was never satisfied. What I expected was something even she, with all her goodwill, could not arrange. I wanted one entire magical day, during which I would live under special dispensation. On my birthday, I thought, nothing bad would be allowed to happen. I would be Queen for a Day, beautiful in a whirly party dress and glossy patent leather shoes, charming as I led my guests through party games, gracious as I opened heaps of presents, all of which would be things I'd always wanted.

I also coveted a surprise party. Everyone else seemed to have one. Year after year, I enviously joined groups hushed in someone's kitchen, or giggling in a large closet, or perhaps openly assembled in a living room, as we all waited for the lucky girl to burst through the door into a fireworks of applause, cheers, and "SURPRISE!" My own birthday fell in early summer, when school was out, friends scattered on vacation, and no one felt like organizing anything. I dropped clumsy hints and then watched gloomily as they sank, shipwrecked bottles with unread messages: "SURPRISE! HAPPY BIRTHDAY!"

Perhaps I wanted a surprise party because then I would not have been responsible for its success. Someone else would have had to worry whether everyone was having a good time. In my quiet childhood, birthday parties were high social events, and children compared details the way in later years young married couples compared gourmet menus. What were the favors at Sally's party? (Oh, yuck, pencils.) Did everyone get prizes for the games? (No, Mary won *two!* It wasn't fair!) Were there really Hershey bars for each guest? (Yes, *and* paper hats, *and* noisemakers, *and* those funny balloons with triple bumps!)

Besides the right balloons and prizes, birthday parties, like all parties, depended upon an unpredictable mix of people, moods, and moments. Some parties sparkled with laughter and excitement; others fizzled. In my self-critical eyes, nothing went right at my own parties. At other people's, the games were more sophisticated, the favors fancier, the laughter louder. Lucky Judy, I groused to myself, she had a roomful of those helium balloons that bump the ceiling when you let them go. Marcia's dad took everyone up for an airplane ride. And for Melissa's seventh birthday, her mom drove everyone in their station wagon to Des Moines, where they all got to have chocolate milk and lemon meringue pie at Bishop's Cafeteria. What can we possibly do to make my party that *special?* So now when Jennifer begins to unravel her own complex and tangled plans, I can hear my long-ago voice through hers: *"Please,* Mother, I want this to be a *good* party."

I want her to have a good party too. So we both hold hopes that are hard to fulfill. On Jennie's last birthday, I vowed to make the dining room, where most of the party would happen, as gala as possible. From the chandelier Jennie and I strung red, purple, and green crepe-paper streamers, twisted into each corner of the room to simulate a circus tent. Multicolored balloons hung in a huge cluster over the table, bobbling slightly in the breeze. Birthday hats, red-and-blue napkins, and matching paper plates transformed the old oak table, and favors peeked enticingly from paper cups. Fumble-fingered as I usually am, I felt proud as we looked at the waving streamers, bobbing balloons, and inviting table. This was it! Backdrop for the birthday party of my dreams! But that, I suddenly realized as I stood in the doorway, basking in self-satisfaction, was the problem. No party could live up to this kind of promise. The room now was empty and silent. In an hour, six girls would be sitting around the table, enjoying themselves — we hoped. But how could they possibly provide the steady continuo of laughter, the happy talk, the sheer hum of excitement, that I envisioned as a necessary background?

And they didn't. Something seemed to go wrong at that party, as though the ghost of Jennie's and my expectations hovered coldly over the pile of presents, the sagging cake, and the flickering candles. Jennie seemed tense, conversation lagged, pauses spread uncomfortably. Several of the games fell flat. "Oh, I've played that before," someone said, "and I didn't like it." Jennie got two games of High-Q, and she already had one on her shelf upstairs. Somebody teased somebody else about her new hairdo, and I had to intervene to stop the tears. Later, after everyone had gone home, Jennie curled up next to me on the sofa. "Mommy, this wasn't a very good birthday," she said sadly. "In fact, I think this was the worst birthday I ever had. I don't know why, it just was."

I thought for a moment before replying. Part of me wanted to launch into my think-of-how-lucky-you-are routine, the lecture that reminds my daughter of her health, good fortune, and loving environment. Part of me wanted to pooh-pooh, saying in a jolly, heartening tone, "Nonsense! Why, this was a terrific party! Everyone had a wonderful time!" But I didn't. I thought of my own birthdays and my childish wish that someone would bring me perfect happiness with a big red bow. I thought of mothers who wanted to give their children that kind of package, even when they knew they couldn't. I thought about impossible dreams. "Yes," I finally said, "I can tell you didn't enjoy yourself as much as you hoped. Some birthdays are like that."

Next year, I thought, we will talk more about desires and disappointments. Next year we will plan more realistically. I will try to care less. And soon, my friends with older children assure me, she will arrange her own parties. She won't want me or my help around at all, and finally she'll give up on the whole idea, probably until she's thirty-nine or has to start worrying about her own children's birthday parties.

If I could go back and celebrate her first ten birthdays again, what would I do differently? Some of my friends, who seem to give birthday parties more easily than I do, helpfully suggest certain rules. Be firm, they say with a confidence I envy. Tell your child how many guests, and what you're willing to do. Specify under two dollars a present, or talk to all the other parents and agree to pass on presents this year. Hire a baby-sitter with a car of her own. Relax! Enjoy yourself! I've tried some of that, I answer meekly, and I didn't do too well. When I said, "Only four guests, Jennie," Jennie thought of six friends who were absolute musts, and I could see her point. The only baby-sitter she wanted doesn't drive. And as for presents! Unless parents know each other well enough to discuss price tags, setting mutual limits is difficult. Can I embarrass Jennie by making her carry just a box of crayons to someone else's party, if everyone else is determined to give stuffed animals? My informants scoffed. "You're just determined not to like birthday parties," one said with asperity.

Perhaps. Not long ago, leafing through a cheerful paperback, *Great Parties for Young Children,* by Cheryl Carter Barron and Cathy Carmichael Scherzer, I could see what I've missed. They obviously enjoy birthday parties, and they have compiled an enthusiastic list of ideas for others to try. Many of their parties have themes, like "Clowns, Clowns, Clowns," "Pet Parade," "Olympiad," "Pow-Wow." Some of these parties take more time to plan and execute than I ever had — I learned years ago to skip instructions that begin "Go to a lumberyard and buy quarter-inch dowels" or include more than one of the following: "glue," "staple," "cut," or "tie" — and per-

haps their children accept their mothers' brightly offered ideas more readily than mine ever did. (She was
*born* humming "I'll do it *my* way.") Nonetheless, Jennie
and I both became interested in the games they suggest,
which include such old favorites as a shoe race, a memory tray, penny pitch, Mother May I? and scavenger
hunts.

Scavenger hunts, I mused longingly. *I* always wanted
a scavenger hunt, I told Jennie, but somehow I never
quite knew how to organize one, or maybe my friends
made faces, or was it that Celia had had one at *her* party
that same spring? Suddenly I was off again, in a make-
believe world of fun and games, seeing myself the center
of a group of happy children, racing from door to door
to collect wooden spoons, candles, Kleenex, and pencils.
The Unforgettable Scavenger Hunt at the Unforgettable Party. Jennie interrupted my fantasy. "I think that
sounds kind of stupid," she said thoughtfully. It was a
true voice from my past. Maybe, I thought, the authors
should have called their book not *Great Parties,* but *Parties
That May Work.* Next year, I said out loud to Jennie,
could we concentrate on having an okay party, and forget about the "great"?

But next year I'll probably blow up all the balloons
again. Like gaily colored invitations hanging in the air,
they will whisper, "Party! Party! Someone's giving a party!"
Fragile and evanescent, they will also remind me that
celebrations do not last, so we must catch what pleasures
we can as they waft by. Finally, I will try not to fill them
so full with Jennie's and my hopes that they burst before
everyone can take one home.

# The Cut-Glass Christmas

THE DECEMBER after my father died, when I was seven and my sister nine, we worried about Mother. We knew she was going to feel badly on Christmas Day, and we wanted to do something special, but we didn't know what. We huddled in the bathroom, whispered in corners, argued intensely in our bedroom after lights out, and, unusually for us, we finally agreed. We would be Mother's Santa; we would fill a stocking for her this year, just as she did for us. How surprised she'd be Christmas morning to see her very own stocking hanging there on the drawer pulls of the maple bureau in our living room! We were sure that would cheer her up.

A week before Christmas, we emptied our piggy banks and set out for Woolworth's, where we always bought our presents. Woolworth's was the Santa-Claus-and-Christmas-tree part of Christmas. It blazed with lights in the after-school dark, smelled of peanuts and popcorn at a counter piled high with chocolate-covered cherries and cellophane-wrapped red-and-white candy canes, rang with "Jingle Bells" and "Hark the Herald Angels Sing" on a radio turned up loud near the cash register. It sparkled with rows of brilliant glass balls, tinsel ropes, and lights that bubbled when you plugged them in.

First we headed for our two traditional counters for

Mother's presents, cosmetics and kitchen utensils. Although Mother never wore makeup, I wouldn't give up hope, encouraging her with a fake tortoiseshell compact of red rouge, or a tiny bottle of Evening in Paris perfume, or a set of mascara brushes. My sister was fond of small silver funnels, metal straining spoons, glass measuring cups. But this Christmas we felt none of our usual gifts would be quite right for a special stocking. We wandered up and down the rows, pondering pencil sharpeners, packaged stationery in floral cardboard boxes, embossed leather billfolds. We rejected a card of assorted needles from England, a fat red pincushion with an attached strawberry-shaped emery ball, an earring tree. The tree was gold-colored metal and spun on a plastic base, but Mother didn't wear earrings.

At last we found ourselves together, discouraged, at a back counter, hidden behind toys and semidarkened under a burned-out fluorescent light, where Woolworth's kept its glasses, dishes, pots and pans. We knew we couldn't afford a teakettle or a frying pan. Mother used empty jam jars for glasses, and she didn't need any more silverware. But suddenly we both saw at the far end of the counter a section of cut-glass dishes, not just plain round cereal bowls, but jagged and deeply carved dark green glass. Small bowls were ten cents, a size big enough for soup or oatmeal was twenty. I picked one up and hurried to the end of the counter where it was brighter. How the glass shone! My sister agreed that the fancy dishes were unlike anything Mother had. With our allowances pooled, we could buy six small bowls and two big ones. The clerk at the front packed the dishes carefully in newspaper and warned us to unpack them gently. The edges were sharp, she said. We hurried home in the dark, happy and warm inside with our secret. Eight cut-glass bowls! Mother would never have had such a Christmas.

On Christmas Eve my sister and I faced our only other problem: what to use for Mother's stocking. We both had red felt Christmas stockings, hung year after year, but we hadn't had enough money to buy one for Mother. While Mother was washing dishes after supper, we tiptoed down the hall into her room and began to rummage through her dresser. Winters were cold in Iowa, and Mother had several pairs of sensible cotton and wool anklets, but none of them seemed big enough. We could barely fit one small bowl into each sock. My sister lifted out a cardboard packet. "What about these?" she said. We looked at each other, then at the beige silky stockings, never worn, folded neatly around the cardboard. Mother didn't have many nylons; this was just a few years after the war, and they were still expensive. But we knew these stockings would be big enough to hold our dishes. "I think if we're careful, it'll be okay," I said. We hurried out of the bedroom with the nylons hidden under my sister's skirt.

Early Christmas morning we crept out of our beds, barely breathing as we passed Mother's door, desperately hoping she wouldn't hear our feet on the creaky wooden stairs. In the living room we hurriedly stuffed her stockings, using both nylons, yanking them wide to accommodate the jagged edges of the cut-glass bowls. We didn't try to hang them up. They were too heavy. Instead we propped them against the bureau that we used for Santa in the absence of a fireplace. Then we looked at the bulging stockings, grinned with pleasure at each other, and ran to the staircase to call Mother.

When Mother sleepily entered the living room, her eyes were immediately riveted to the bureau. Two green cut-glass bowls hung precariously over the tops of her stretched, snagged, new nylon stockings. "My," she said. "Did you girls do all this?" There was something odd in her tone, but she quickly recovered. "What absolutely beautiful bowls," she said admiringly, sitting down on the floor and taking them out, one by one, setting them in a row on the floor for us all to enjoy. She hugged us both. We were so proud we had pleased her. "You are wonderful girls to have thought of this, and I love you both very much," she said. She ignored the empty stockings sagging on the floor beside her.

Now a mother myself, living alone with an eight-year-old daughter, at Christmas I think of many things, but always I remember that Christmas of the cut-glass bowls. To me it shines as a beacon my mother left me, a beacon to guide me through the maze of conflicting feelings, emotional demands, free-floating guilt and worry that afflict me at Christmas. When my mother looked at those ruined stockings and ugly cut-glass bowls, which eventually disappeared into the deep recesses of her bottom shelves, she knew what Christmas was all about: "I love you both very much."

It is often hard for me to remember what Christmas is all about. As a teacher on the semester plan, I always find myself buried under term papers and final examinations just before Christmas, a weight that may not be lifted until New Year's, when grades are irrevocably due. Meanwhile a mountain of mail begins to build up on my dining room table, aunts, cousins, dear old friends, all of whom need to hear from me. I have presents to wrap, hurriedly, at the last minute. My daughter has sudden desperate desires to make things; the tree needs to be planted firmly in its stand, lighted, decorated; where are the candles that always go on the mantel? Marking a paper with red pencil, trying to stay within the margins and be helpful but not unkind, I throw it down on the floor when the phone rings. Can we come to Sunday brunch across town? Will I bring a salad? I have no time at Christmas, no time at all.

So I try to think of the cut-glass bowls. I put Christmas

carols on the hi-fi ("Play 'Rudolph the Red-Nosed Reindeer' again, Mommy") and sit down to examine my own priorities. What do I want out of Christmas? What does it mean to me at the heart of the rustling tissue paper, blinking lights, ringing phone? What must I find time to do? As I listen to the familiar carols, my mind begins to clear. I realize first that Christmas means, oddly enough, silence. At Christmas I feel more than ever a need to get away from myself, from others, and listen to the quiet. I find myself taking long walks after dark, walking by my neighbors' houses, looking at their trees blazing in the windows, admiring the cheerful displays on their outdoor evergreens. I listen to the crackle of frosty branches in the wind, the crunch of my footsteps on the ice, my own moist breath as I puff into a wool scarf with the faint smell of mothballs.

On a cold, bright night when the stars are out above the city, and the remaining elms on our street cast strange dark patterns on the white snow, it seems to me while I walk that I can listen to passing time. I can almost hear the year slipping by. I don't much like New Year's Eve, I stay home in indignant protest against being automatically forced to stay up until midnight, I remember New Year's Day as a heavy, sleepy, soggy day of ham, beer, football games, and exhaustion. But at Christmas I do my thinking about the coming year, and I watch the old one go. Perhaps because we often remember past Christmases, their hopes and disappointments, our childhoods stretching out behind us, we can have at Christmas an uncanny sense of where we are and where we may be going. I always feel a little sad, recalling past losses and failures, but then I think of what we celebrate at Christmas, a birth and a new beginning, and I am comforted. I can almost feel hope in the air and see it sparkle in the lighted trees. As I step back into my warm little house, I don't feel so cross. I have another chance. Next year maybe I will do better.

One of the ways I find time to *think* about time in the midst of the rushed holidays is by going to at least one concert. Somehow I always manage to squeeze in an afternoon or an evening of Christmas music, probably *The Messiah,* but chamber music or a cantata by my favorite local choir will do as well. For two or three hours I am at peace, letting my mind wander among the harmonies of Handel or Bach. Of course I am bombarded by so-called Christmas music everywhere, in shopping centers, in restaurants, on television, but I never feel the season is complete until I have sat quietly, in a darkened hall, and traveled back to share earlier affirmations of Christmas joy. The jarring dissonance of my life is rearranged for that brief time into order and resolution.

The deepest source of peace may be inside a church. I feel I would lose Christmas entirely if I could not share in at least one church service of the season. Once I stayed away from Christmas services for several years after hearing an irritable minister inveigh against those of us he called "Christmas tourists," who never came to church at other times and who seldom financially supported the church that took them in at holidays. But, guilty though I sometimes feel about my transience, I was eventually driven back. Though far from orthodox, I am still moved by the simple words of the King James version of the Nativity, its promise and hope. I avoid the grandiose city churches with their paid choirs, forests of poinsettias, and ministers skilled in the jargon of encounter groups. Instead I flee to a small family church, to a service unpopular because it is held at the cocktail hour. There I am pleased if I can see a straw crèche, sing "Silent Night" and "It Came upon a Midnight Clear," light a small candle myself and hold it briefly aloft, a token of continuing faith that somehow, somewhere, all will be well.

Deep in the quiet of church, or at a concert, or walking down my street at night, I let my mind wander over the past. There I always meet old friends and invent conversations with them, trying to imagine what they look like now, asking them how they are doing. That is why I use Christmas as a time to restore damaged or dying relationships. During the holidays I recklessly run up my phone bill to call distant friends I'm worried about. What is Joyce doing in Richmond? Is Sally lonely this Christmas in London? Why haven't I heard from Lynda in Vancouver? Has Larry recovered from his mother's death? I have been known to startle an old lover who thought he was well rid of me by calling him after four years at Christmas to ask how he was, how are the children, do they visit often, is he happy? Such a call can lay an unhappy ghost finally and completely to rest. Then for weeks during January I answer my cards, glue snapshots of my daughter on top of printed messages, write short letters, ask a few questions that may only be answered next Christmas when the cards come again. One year my favorite Christmas card simply said, "Of all things this coming year be careful of love." At Christmas I try to keep the small flames glowing on candles that may be burning out for want of care.

Perhaps as part of my wish to reaffirm bonds at Christmas, I also make some time in my kitchen, baking special treats to share with others. I study glossy pictures in magazines, clip recipes, read them to myself at night in bed. If I didn't have a full-time job, I fantasize, I could spend the whole month creating gingerbread houses, turning out dozens of decorated cookies, rush from door to door with loaves of swirled, candied, beraisined bread. As it is I usually have to settle for one long Saturday morning surrounded by spotted, yellowing recipes never used; cake flour that seems a suspicious antique gray; fancy molds dug out from cobwebbed corners. Last year it was plum pudding, from scratch, with as many jeweled fruits as I could stuff into the batter — three plum puddings, actually, since my molds were all rather small. We ate one Christmas Day, gave one away to friends to take home, shared another with neighbors later in the week. For days after the actual baking smells were gone, an aroma of warmth and sweetness seemed to linger in my kitchen.

I am always tired after Christmas. Sometimes I get cranky, catch cold, come down with a headache; signs of stress, I do not need to be told. It may be foolish to try to cram so much into an already bursting schedule, to sandwich concerts around exams to be graded, plum pudding between cards to be answered, a long walk under starlight when presents are waiting to be wrapped. But I cannot bring myself to give up any more of Christmas than I am absolutely forced to. I fervently pack it all in as my sister and I stuffed those glass dishes into Mother's stretching nylons so many Christmases ago. Like my mother, I want to set out the tokens of love on the living room floor, look past their gaudy color and cut-glass gleam, ignore the ruined stockings that held them, and remember why they are there.

# My New Year's Resolution: A Shorter List

 WHEN I WAS GROWING UP, New Year's Eves came slowly and far apart. Each day was a lifetime, and each month lasted forever. In December I had endless weeks of anticipating Christmas, decorating the tree, wrapping gifts, cutting out sugar cookies, caroling, lighting candles on Christmas Eve, heaping hard sauce on my plum pudding. During the week following Christmas, I gradually focused on the astonishing fact that December 31 was approaching — 1952 was about to become 1953, or 1960 would soon disappear into 1961. Some changes were more marked than others; when I was nine, and the world prepared to enter 1950, I was dazzled by *Life*'s speculation about what small-letter "life" might be like in the year 2000. I couldn't even say the words "two thousand" to myself without a shiver, partly from a flood of bizarre images from science-fiction movies, partly from my disbelief that I could ever live to be that old, partly because the intervening years seemed like a promise of near-immortality.

Now I watch the coming new year with a different kind of amazement. I have barely gotten used to writing 1986 on my checks. Sometimes, because time passes so quickly, I can't instantly remember how old I am; I stop to subtract 1940, a nice round number, from the current date in order to find out. Once a few months ago, when my mind was flitting among myriad distractions, I started to do this calculation and realized I had actually forgotten, for a few terrifying moments, what year it was.

So it seems like only yesterday that I made my last set of New Year's resolutions. I don't do it formally anymore. As a child and even into young adulthood, when I had a firmer belief in sudden change and in the magical powers of lists, I wrote my resolutions down on paper. Fortunately, I never saved those recorded scraps of good intentions. They would probably have the same haunting flatness, the lack of a sense of past or future, of the few diary entries I made from time to time — usually starting with the New Year, when someone had given me a diary for Christmas, and ending a week or two later with unilluminating lines like "Saw Bob Callahan and Don Soults at the movies today. I think Bob likes Celia."

Those New Year's resolutions of younger days undoubtedly covered now-familiar dissatisfactions with myself, uneasiness about my moral life, and hopes for renewed discipline: "Go on diet." "Go to church every Sunday." "Keep room clean." "Write in diary." "Work on Camp Fire Good Citizenship Badge." The words would be different today, but the basic impulses remain: Go on diet. Meditate regularly. Clean closets. Write every day. Make a difference.

Why do I no longer make a list? First, the words look too simple. I'm aware now that nothing is simple. What kind of diet? How serious? Calorie-counting, Weight Watchers, or positive thinking? Meditate when? If I go to church and do my t'ai chi and walk around the lake, do I still need to meditate that day? Shouldn't I put off cleaning my closets until I've reglued the wallpaper in the bathroom and repotted the fig tree? How can I write when I have migraines or blue books to grade? What can I actually *do* to make a difference?

141

And maybe I'm tired of so many new starts. After all, it isn't just New Year's that reminds me of passing time, unfulfilled promises, and new opportunities. When my teaching year ends in May, I look ahead to the summer and reassess my life: what should I do with this gift of free time? In June, I have a birthday. Again? What happened to forty-five? Where do I want to be at forty-seven? In September, when classes start, I am stimulated by the excitement of returning students to begin planning my own new schedule, laying out my course, deciding how to allot my time outside the classroom. With the fresh brisk winds of fall, I feel the hope of new beginnings. What wonders I will accomplish this semester! And then suddenly it's Christmas, and New Year's.

Perhaps I have gradually had to recognize that change is slow, never steady, and sometimes almost impossible. If I've never been as thin as a *Vogue* model, do I really think it will happen now? Have my closets ever been neat and spartan? Is my racing mind likely to sink into the deep-breathing rhythms of a tranquil guru? I don't want to give up, but maybe I've learned to hope for more modest results. No desserts at lunch! Fill up a bag for the Free Store! Get back to t'ai chi class once a month! March with Mothers Against Drunk Driving!

Without a written list of last year's promises to myself, I don't have to blame myself for breaking any. I don't want to concentrate on failures. Looking back on the past year, I instead pat myself on the back for having done what I could. For driving again, occasionally and for short distances, on freeways. For writing a piece about something I didn't want to talk about. For (almost) not nagging my daughter about her room (quite so much). None of these efforts looks very impressive on paper; maybe that's why I don't write them down.

As I look ahead to the new year, I also know what I couldn't when I was young: the future is absolutely unpredictable. No one can guarantee me — or those I love — health, success, or happiness, no matter how many resolutions we make or keep or break. I can only resolve to do my best at the time, to forgive myself if I don't, and to hope for a chance to try again. Day by day, I can remind myself to pay attention to what matters, but on each day, that may be different. Not bound by a list, I'm better equipped to stay loose. So all I'm writing on my mental tablet this year is: take a deep breath, smile when you can, and keep moving. Nineteen eighty-seven, here I come, one more time!

# SIX

# *Watching Out for Real Writers*

# Watching Out for Real Writers

"NOW THERE'S a Real Writer," said my dinner partner, admiringly. He was speaking about a nationally published novelist who had given a lecture on writing that my dinner partner had attended. "I do some writing myself," my new friend confessed, "but I realized after hearing him that I'll never make it." "Why not?" I asked. "Because he explained that a Real Writer sits at his typewriter or desk every day, for at least four hours, writing something. It doesn't much matter what, it's a question of just doing it. Keeping the wheels oiled and so on. No matter what your other priorities are, you simply make room for those three or four hours. And I guess I don't always do that."

"Well," I said gloomily, "neither do I." We were both silent for a few minutes. I felt a familiar guilt, sinking heavily enough into my stomach so that I actually passed the strawberry shortcake to my neighbor without a second helping. I should have tried to cheer him up, but he had unknowingly hit me in a vulnerable spot: my fear that I, too, will never be a Real Writer. Perhaps because I did not begin writing stories and essays until my mid-thirties, I still feel tentative about describing myself as a writer. I do write, but I do other things too, and I never know quite which person to put first on any particular day. Today am I Susan Toth the writer, or

147

the teacher, or the mother, or the gardener, or the housekeeper, or the chauffeur, or . . . ? Many women, and men, with multiple lives face this dilemma of priorities. My difficulty in boldly stating that I am in fact a writer is, however, compounded by what I have begun to realize is a powerful and pernicious myth. I call it the Myth of the Real Writer.

Nurtured by successful writers who like to moralize about how they got where they are, and by unsuccessful writers who justify their continued efforts by identifying themselves as privileged members of a demanding and elite society, the Myth of the Real Writer obviously has a purpose. It informs aspirants to this closed circle about whether they are worthy and instructs them about how they may achieve acceptance. It also effectively discourages some would-be Real Writers from seriously writing at all, thus lessening the competition. Those of us who do not fit the pattern the Myth prescribes should perhaps examine it more closely.

First, the Myth says, Real Writers start early. They begin writing poetry in kindergarten on bits of construction paper, sandwich short stories among their junior-high notebooks, and sometime in their teens probably begin a novel. (After becoming famous, one needs lots of juvenilia to publish.) In college they belong to a creative-writers' club and probably edit a literary magazine. By their twenties, they work most nights and rainy weekends on a second or third novel. As they approach thirty, by the sheer accumulation of years of writing, they have become Real Writers. When you meet them at a reading or a party, it is hard not to feel daunted. My advice is to stare them down and think very hard about a varied assortment of late starters, like Laurence Sterne, George Eliot, Laura Ingalls Wilder, or even the immensely successful Helen Van Slyke. Start collecting names of other

148

late starters, and add them to your list. Recite the list silently under your breath whenever you feel old.

The second article of the Myth of the Real Writer is that he/she always belongs to a writers' group, or, more precisely, a Real Writers' Group. Here everyone allegedly shares rapt attention, constructive criticism, and friendly support. Well, maybe. (It's important to remember that the Myth does work for some writers.) But writing for me is an intensely solitary activity. I sit down at a typewriter with images and vaguely shaped ideas, and I write until they have worked themselves out in words. I have never wanted to read a piece of my writing aloud until it was finished and polished, and then I pick my critics very, very carefully. I prefer a far-off editor's comments; a fellow writer has an overwhelming involvement in his/her own subject matter, point of view, and style. Although I like my writer friends, I don't really want to read their preliminary work, and I suspect they are not terribly anxious to read mine.

Not only do Real Writers belong to writers' groups, but they also keep journals. They not only keep them, but they talk a lot about keeping them. Real Writers read to each other from their journals, mention urgent entries they made at 2 A.M. last night, knowingly remark how so-and-so's story is just like a idea in his/her journal last November. Rather than immersing themselves in Shakespeare, Yeats, or Dickens, some take courses in journal writing instead. Although I very occasionally jot down notes for a story in a notebook if I don't have time to work an idea out at the moment, I usually find that when I get back to my notebook, the ephemeral feelings associated with my notes have vanished like a magical mist. With them has vanished the story. The notebook isn't much comfort. A few times in my life I've tried to keep a daily diary, but I've always given up after a week or two. So when Real Writers earnestly ask me about my journal, I am embarrassed; I feel I can hardly be a Real Writer without one.

And finally, as my dinner partner reminded me, Real Writers write every day. I don't. I cannot always clear my mind to match the clear spaces on my sheet of typing paper. Tillie Olson has written eloquently about the conflict between family life and "participation in life as a human being" on the one hand, and urgent creative impulse on the other. Neither she nor anyone else I know has ever given me a satisfactory solution on how to assess priorities. No question so terrifies me as "What are you working on now?" Sometimes I am not working on anything. Sometimes I am holding myself together with safety pins, or grading papers, or cleaning my basement. "At the moment," I sometimes want to tell my questioner, "I am not writing. I am merely living." Merely? Is that what I heard myself say? Over my shoulder I glance to see if a Real Writer is listening, taking notes for his journal, preparing a story for his writers' group, or heading for his daily four-hour stint at the typewriter. At least if the Real Writer has left for a while, taking the Myth with him, I can help myself to his piece of the strawberry shortcake.

# "If You're a Writer,
# Why Aren't You Writing?"

WHEN I HEAR generalizations about "the creative life," I tend to glaze over. If artists are talking, they often become righteous and aggrieved, and so I stop listening. If others are solemnly discussing artists, they make the species sound so rarefied, with strange markings, unpredictable habits, and a frightening drift toward extinction, that I'm soon convinced I don't want to be included. But at certain times I do my own share of philosophizing about "the creative life." I usually worry about it when I'm not having one.

When I was asked to ponder "the needs of the individual artist," I had at first my usual uneasy reaction. Worse, as I thought further, the scope of the assignment seemed overwhelming. How could I, a writer, possibly imagine what a sculptor needs most, or a filmmaker, or a dancer? Then, not long afterward, at the end of a frustrating day when I had intended to return to a long-abandoned story, I found myself snapping at my husband and daughter, who were being heartlessly cheerful at the dinner table. "Oh, it's all very well for you," I grumbled. "I had a lousy day. I had hoped to get some writing done, and I didn't. I don't think I'll ever write again. I don't even think I'm a writer anymore. I'm just a teacher, mother, cook, chauffeur, you name it — anything but a writer!"

"How come?" asked my husband reasonably. I snorted and got up to pour the coffee, scraping my chair disagreeably and slamming the cups on the counter to avoid answering. I found myself asking that question again. How come? What *did* I need that I wasn't getting? I couldn't speak for all artists, but I could certainly speak for myself. What did it take for me to lead an artistic life — or, stated less pompously, to get my writing done?

When teaching full-time, which I usually am, I knew the most important answer. Time. What I, and any artist, need most of all is time. Physically and mentally exhausted after a day in the classroom, I find it impossible to work intellectually at anything else. Sometimes I snatch a few hours on Saturday and Sunday, but during a week's interruption, I can't always sustain an inspiration, an idea, or even the careful development of a paragraph. When I return, whatever had begun to flower on the page has withered. And I am luckier than most, holding a job that allows me long vacation breaks several times a year. I thought of Tillie Olson's anguished essay, "Silences," in which she describes the creative agony of being "always used by the writing, always denied." When finally she got the time she needed, she felt it was perhaps too late: "I could manage only the feeblest, shallowest growth on that devastated soil. Weeds, to be burned like weeds, or used as compost. . . . Work interrupted, deferred, relinquished, makes blockage — at best, lesser accomplishment. Unused capacities atrophy, cease to be."

What do my artist friends wish for most? Not necessarily money, but time. Money is important because it *buys* time. One friend, a photographer, seldom complains about her antiquated equipment or her inability to travel or her rare contacts with other photographers. Rather, she complains about lack of time. On weekends, she is buried in her darkroom, but all too soon Monday mornings, and her necessary job, signal the end of whatever project she has just begun. "If only I had the time . . . ," many of us sigh to each other.

We measure available grants not by dollars, but by the time they can create. Grateful as we are for an award of $100 or $250 or a "seed" grant of, say, $2,500, it doesn't buy much time. In my own state of Minnesota, one program offers individual artist's grants of $25,000, and most of us dream of those. We are greedy not for big bucks, but for the chunks of time grants will buy — and that sum buys enough time to finish something.

"At least I have a darkroom to escape into," my photographer friend says, finding comfort where she can. That is clearly another necessity. An artist needs space to work. For me, a writer, that simply means an orderly space. A table. An electric connection for my word processor. Light and ventilation so I do not wilt too quickly. Running water nearby so I don't have any excuses to leave. A quiet environment so I can hear myself think, letting words and sentences fall into a receptive silence until they can slowly settle into their proper place. Usually I can find a suitable room almost anywhere, if I can manage to enforce quiet. For other artists, needs of space are more complicated: a studio large enough to hang a giant canvas, or to hold a kiln, blocks of stone, buckets of paint, cement, film canisters, tools. Like time, a room of one's own costs money.

Money cannot provide every artist's needs as simply as buying time and space, however. Most of us need an audience. Emily Dickinson may have been able to keep writing poems while stuffing them unseen into a drawer, but all writers are not made of her stern moral fiber. We want readers. As we write, we want our words to reach across separating space and connect us to others who will understand, and thus validate, what we are saying. We grow discouraged without readers, and many of us give up. Painters want someone to admire their paintings, filmmakers want their films shown and discussed, dancers want to dance before an audience.

An audience for one's work can bring a work to fruition. When I was in the midst of my first book, *Blooming: A Small-Town Girlhood,* I wasn't sure — and neither was my first agent — that anyone would want to read it when and if it was ever finished. I had begun writing only in my mid-thirties, and I felt quite abashed about describing myself as a "real" writer. Although I had published some stories and essays, this was my first full-length project. It was scary. Friends and colleagues wanted to encourage me, but often their faces showed disbelief and concern when I told them what I was doing. "*What* did you say you're writing?" they asked. "A book about growing up in Iowa in the fifties? So what's the story in *that*?" Less troublesome, but hardly supportive, responses were: "No kidding." "Huh." "How about that." "Well, well." "You don't say." When I received my first important grant, an award from the Minnesota State Arts Board that enabled me to take a leave from teaching and finish the book, I was buoyed not only by the money, important as that was, but by the vote of confidence it represented. A handful of competent critics had decided that my book was worth finishing — and reading. That knowledge strengthened my spirits on bleak days.

But finding, or providing, an audience isn't simple. Not long ago I attended a meeting of writers who were trying to give local foundations a list of their needs as a guide to general planning. Many of the writers wanted, quite naturally, more readers. Why not subsidize small magazines? they asked. Provide newspaper space for short stories? Publish broadsides of poems to be sold at the state fair? Buy radio time for new work to be read? The writers at my table were ingenious and creative in their ideas. But even as I brainstormed with them, a tiny voice in the back of my mind — sounding very much like my aunt Isabel in Winnetka — said with asperity, "But suppose I don't *want* to read that young woman's poetry? What then?" It wasn't Aunt Isabel's voice, of course; it was my own. A few weeks before the meeting, I had served on an awards committee that read almost a hundred manuscripts. Some were marvelous, intriguing, and inventive. Others, not surprisingly, were dull, banal, and imitative. "Why should *anyone* have to read this stuff?" I'd asked myself more than once.

Now, in the planning meeting, I noticed we were all assuming that any writer — which seemed to mean anyone who wrote, no matter how or what — deserved to have readers. In the beleaguered, frustrated tone around me, I could also detect the sense that if writers were missing their audience, it was clearly the fault of the undereducated, insensitive, reactionary public — not the writers. As I listened more carefully, I became disturbed. "The average middle-class guy, the TV watcher, isn't going to get this anyway," I heard someone say. "Well, we're not writing for *them*," someone else added. One well-known populist writer spoke eloquently about the moral superiority of the artist, who was the only segment of society that might save us from the apocalypse. "The public," she pointed out, "will always be blind. They need us to show them the light." Finally I got courage to say, "You know, I'm bothered about all this *us* and *them*, and aren't they us? I'm really not sure that artists are necessarily as morally superior as everyone here seems to think. And taking that attitude of superiority is going to alienate any audience we might have, except each other."

Silence fell. Several writers looked at me in disbelief. I felt as stuffy as my aunt Isabel. Folding my arms, I tried not to look defensive, but I knew I was vulnerable. I had published several pieces in large-circulation magazines, and one of my colleagues present had once commented to another, who in the manner of writers obligingly reported the remark to me, that he was afraid I was in danger of becoming "popular." An older poet, little published, but much respected, looked sternly at me. "You've missed the point," he said. "We need funds to get audiences. They're just not going to appear on their own."

I didn't know how to reply to the poet. Even though he and I agreed that writers needed readers, we were clearly headed for trouble on what followed next. With provocative clarity, Thoreau once provided a list of basic human needs and proposed reasonable, thoughtful solutions. Filling an artist's needs is more complex. We all have a right to decent food, clothing, and shelter. But does every artist have a right to an audience? Does everyone who writes a poem deserve to have that poem read? If an artist can't find an audience, is he or she to blame, rather than the audience? But who is to decide whose work should be seen or heard or experienced? Who will say what kinds of work are encouraged? Who can assuredly know where the problem lies? We needed Thoreau's wisdom at our meeting, though his answers would undoubtedly have made us all uncomfortable.

Some needs cannot be filled by dollars. Even with time, space, and an audience, an artist does not always create. On the evening when I pondered my husband's query about why I wasn't writing, I realized that no grants organization could solve the problem that perenially confronts me. I was at that moment on sabbatical leave, so I had time. I had recently unpacked my boxes and papers in a new study, with a door that locked, so I had space. After two books, I was reasonably confident of an audience. But I was struggling with another need, one much harder to define or solve.

Besides writing, I need to live. I therefore have trouble with priorities. On a day when I am free to write, I do not always write. Sometimes I plant morning glories, or put away clothes, or lunch with a friend, or walk around a nearby lake. I tell myself my latent mind is writing anyway, but my conscience is still assaulted by the voices of the many professional writers who tell interviewers how sternly they hew to their four, six, eight, or even ten hours a day. I envy their resolve, but I don't always have it. Life calls to me seductively, and some days I don't put up much of a struggle. No one ties me to my typewriter as Odysseus' sailors tied him to the mast. I hear a song, and I leap overboard, paddling madly to a concert or movie or picnic or even (I must be honest, even if trivial) to a garage sale.

Sometimes I don't write because I don't have anything to write about. For weeks, sometimes months, I find my creative sources silent. It's not that my Muse is angry, but often she is worn out. She takes a vacation. After each book, for example, I have waited a long time to begin writing again. Eventually I find myself becoming so irritable and cranky that I have to force myself to sit down at the keyboard again. I won't feel whole until I do. But meanwhile I have spent a lot of time filling personal, not artistic, needs. Although I envy the productivity of the writers who turn out one good book a year, or even two, I have resigned myself to my own rhythms: when I die, I tell myself, I'll probably have less on the shelf, more in the garden.

No one can help me with priorities, or inner drive, or even ideas. Those I have to find for myself. No one else can free me from my distractions (and I am not always sure I want to be freed). I was reminded that a writer is someone who writes when I received last week a letter from a woman I'd met after a reading. She has a daughter, Margie, now twenty-five, she said in her letter, who has talent as a writer. "But although Margie's creative-writing teacher told her she should continue, she hasn't," the mother complained. "She has a job in a bank and doesn't seem to care that she's not writing at all. I don't know how to encourage her. Please read these and see what you think." The mother enclosed several manuscripts. I sighed, but eventually replied, in as gentle words as possible, that whether or not her mother or I thought Margie should be a writer was irrelevant. That was really up to Margie. Maybe she was happy at her post at the bank. Writing was hard work, I said, and I could understand if Margie didn't want to do it. I did not ask if Margie needed more money or time or space or audience. First, I felt, Margie needs passionate commitment. Then we could worry about filling her artistic needs.

So sometimes I need, more than anything else, to remind myself of my own commitment to writing. I have to ask myself — or have someone else ask me — why I'm not practicing the craft I have chosen. Yes, I often long for time, space, and a receptive audience. I need money to provide some of those essentials. But I cannot always place the burden of making me a writer on someone, or something, beyond myself.

# E. B. White

    I DIDN'T fall in love with E. B. White immedi-
ately. It was a slow process, beginning in my twenties and maturing as my life grew harder and more
complex. He was there at different times when I needed
him, and, like many readers who were saddened by his
recent death, I wish I could have thanked him properly.

"Love" can be a facile word, and I don't sling it about
easily. In fact, applied to a writer I never met, it may
sound goopy, but it seems to be what I mean, and E. B.
White believed in saying what you mean. I was a passionate admirer both of his writing and of the sensibility
it revealed. He made me feel I knew enough of his
personality — his joys and fears, quirks and constan-
cies — so I might be able to tell him freely all about mine
and he would understand. Of course, despite his ap-
parent openness, his style never became embarrassingly
personal, and he did not invite intrusion. Before his
death, I would have worried that some clipping service
might send him these printed words and make him wince.

I was too old to grow up with E. B. White's classic
children's stories, and I was too young to follow his early
career in the *New Yorker*. I first remember the clear pleasant shock of his prose when I was twenty-three, just out
of graduate school, teaching "A Slight Sound at Evening" from a freshman anthology. Written in contem-

plation and praise of Henry David Thoreau, this essay
is a wonderful mixture of Thoreau, *Walden,* and White.
Although I thought I was quite grown up, what with
being newly married, dressing in a professional-woman's
suit and high heels, and formally lecturing to students,
in fact I fit exactly into the category White describes as
an ideal reader of *Walden:*

> I think it is of some advantage to encounter the book
> at a period in one's life when the normal anxieties and
> enthusiasms and rebellions of youth closely resemble those
> of Thoreau in that spring of 1845 when he borrowed
> an ax, went out to the woods, and began to whack down
> some trees for timber. Received at such a juncture, the
> book is like an invitation to life's dance, assuring the
> troubled recipient that no matter what befalls him in the
> way of success or failure he will always be welcome at
> the party — that the music is played for him, too, if he
> will but listen and move his feet.

Reading these words, I heard E. B. White speaking di-
rectly to me, and somehow I began to recall *Walden* in
a newly personal way.

It was not just that White was giving me a gentle push,
reminding me that life was full of excitement if I paid
attention to the right things. I think now that my pleasure sprang more from what White was doing in his essay,
how as a writer he was using *Walden.* As a serious student
of literature, I had of course "studied" this American
classic. My professors had solemnly discussed Thoreau's
transcendental background, philosophy, and personal
life. One had even uttered solemnities about Thoreau's
style, pointing out metaphors, allusions, and etymolo-
gies. But no one had been *excited* about Thoreau. No
one gave me reasons for why I, or anyone else, felt our
hearts beat faster when we read him. White did. *Walden*

had mattered to him, and he was putting down, lucidly and unashamedly, exactly why.

In the first sentence of "A Slight Sound at Evening," White quotes Thoreau: "In his journal for July 10–12, 1841, Thoreau wrote, 'A slight sound at evening lifts me up by the ears, and makes life seem inexpressibly serene and grand. It may be in Uranus, or it may be in the shutter.' The book into which he later managed to pack both Uranus and the shutter was published in 1854. . . ." Immediately I knew White was on to something. One of the things I had marveled at in *Walden* was its unexpectedness, the way Thoreau catapulted his reader from a bean field into the trajectory of a planet. Although I could not have explained this to myself at twenty-three, I must have already then believed that life is wildly unpredictable, full of quirkiness, snatching us at any moment from the sublime and dumping us unceremoniously into the ridiculous. Thoreau knew that. So did White, for he delighted in the way Thoreau could be equally moved by a sound in the heavens — or in the shutter.

White wrote like that too. On the day he died, I happened to be teaching "The Ring of Time," which is about many things (as are all of White's best essays): the quick passage of time, the gift of sudden moments of happiness, White's melancholy at man's stupidity and prejudice. It was written during the dark period of desegregation in the South in the 1950s, and White was troubled. But in the midst of all this are a few comments on the effects of intense humidity in Florida. White casually mentions that "the newspaper, with its headlines about integration, wilts in your hand and falls limply into the coffee and the egg. Envelopes seal themselves. Postage stamps mate with one another as shamelessly as grasshoppers." I laughed out loud when I read the sentence about the grasshoppers. Pointing to this passage,

I said that this was White's genius. "I don't get it," said one student sourly. "What's so great about postage stamps sticking to each other?"

It was a fair question, and later I tried to frame an answer. It had to do with White's awareness of absurdity in the midst of importance and of how easily human beings are distracted by weather, inconvenience, and the usual vicissitudes of living. It also had to do with his *noticing* how postage stamps stick together on humid days and then effortlessly inventing a commonsense but enchanting simile about it.

When I was twenty-three, I didn't think about White's approach to life. I enjoyed his essay on *Walden* and went on to expound Faulkner's "The Bear" to my freshman class. (They liked him better than White; surface difficulty, for them, was synonymous with importance.) Time passed. I kept finding White's essays in anthologies; I discovered his essential guide for writers, *The Elements of Style*; one day I read *Charlotte's Web* to my young daughter. By the time I picked up a secondhand copy of *The Second Tree from the Corner*, I was hooked. When his *Collected Letters* appeared in 1980, they only confirmed my belief that E. B. White could make life dance in language to any tune he chose.

Writing essays myself, I often hear White's voice in the back of my mind. Although no one can imitate the uncanny lilt of his sentences, a beginning writer can learn from White to trust the sound of his or her own speaking voice. Together with Sarah Orne Jewett, a nineteenth-century writer who also lived much of her life in Maine, White was the greatest influence on my own prose. (He and Jewett also eventually led me to the rocky coast of Maine, something else I have to thank him for.)

As I grew older, I appreciated White even more. His essays never gave easy answers or boringly predictable responses to difficulties. He knew that life does not always end happily, and he didn't pretend otherwise — notice the muted conclusions of *Charlotte's Web* and *Stuart Little* — but he never gave up, either. In the midst of sadness, he found moments of irrepressible joy. After years of teaching and reviewing contemporary literature, I sometimes feel whenever I open a new book that I am about to sink into the seductive muck of despair. Reading E. B. White, or even thinking about him, is a lifeline back to sanity, hope, and laughter.

A few years ago I came across a critical analysis of White by Wilfred Sheed. Not only did Sheed think White was overrated, a minor talent who had never successfully completed a "big novel," but he pointed out that White, often praised for his stability and serenity, was highly neurotic. He cited passages from biography and letters to show that White was often assailed by anxiety, refused to appear in public to give talks or accept awards, consulted psychiatrists at different times in his life, evidently even suffered vague "nervous breakdowns."

Sheed might have thought these revelations would alienate White's admirers. Actually, they had the opposite effect on me. He made White seem both more profound and more accessible. Perhaps I had thought of White as too perfect and too sane. White's obvious courage touched me too; I know something about fear myself. If White could battle with it so gallantly over his long life, his writing drew on even deeper sources of strength than I had imagined. Here is White in a letter describing "a nervous crack-up which visited me last summer and which has given me a merry chase. . . . Doctors weren't much help, but I found that old phonograph records are marvelous. If you ever bust up from nerves, take frequent shower baths, drink dry sherry in small amounts, spend most of your time with hand tools at a bench, and play old records till there is no wax left in the grooves." Lack of self-pity, self-effacing irony, and the zest in his prose make this report hopeful rather than depressing.

Thinking of White as a man who knew fear, anxiety, and self-doubt, but who still reveled in life, I continue to want him as a guide. It is not easy to try to write prose, or live a life, with his humor, resilience, and staying power. But White's essays, stories, and letters reaffirm the "invitation to life's dance" and tell the reader "that the music is played for him, too, if he will but listen and move his feet." I was always an awkward dancer, but listening to E. B. White, I plan to go on trying to move my feet.

# The Importance of
# Being Remembered

THE PHONE RANG. Stirring a pot of sticky
green pea soup with one hand, I grabbed the re-
ceiver with the other. "Is this Sue Allen from Ames,
Iowa?" a deep voice asked over long-distance crackling.
"Yes," I said, knees beginning to quiver. I knew what
he was going to say next, and he did: "This is a voice
out of your past." A little laugh, then an awkward silence.
Whoever was calling had obviously just read one of my
two memoirs. *Blooming* covers my childhood in Ames,
Iowa, in the 1940s and 1950s; *Ivy Days* continues through
Smith College and graduate school. Both end more than
twenty years ago. "Do you know who this is?" the voice
went on, nudging. "No, I'm afraid I don't," I answered
apologetically. I somehow felt I *ought* to know. "Well,
this is Brian Beeman. I've just read your book, and I
wanted to call up and say hello."

Though I hadn't thought about him since I graduated
from Ames High in 1957, I remembered Brian Beeman.
He handled sound effects for Drama Club, and so we
shared insider jokes, gossip, an occasional pizza, and
rides home. He was odd, often harsh and acerbic, and
something of a loner. "Brian!" I said now, with a sense
of something dim dropping into my kitchen and beginning to brighten, like a cinematic visitor from outer space:
"Of course! Where are you? Tell me about yourself!"

165

While he talked, I stirred the split pea soup. Then Brian startled me again: "Tell me, Sue," he asked without warning, "are you happy?"

In a few minutes I had let the soup burn on the bottom. Trying to answer, I found myself wallowing in inanities, approximations, and qualifiers. Brian still knew how to make me uncomfortable. After he had hung up, I scrubbed out the soup pot. But I was no longer in my kitchen. I had plunged back into the anticipatory darkness of the high-school auditorium, seeing Brian's pale sharp face staring at me from the wings; at the same time I was thinking distractedly about whether I was happy. I was awash once more in the inescapable wake of writing a memoir. What happens afterward is much like what happens during the writing: you are forced to make connections to people you had long forgotten and to reconsider your life.

For months after each book appeared, I was off balance. At a book signing in Des Moines, a portly, balding, middle-aged man in tennis sweater and baggy pants strode up to me with a confident smile. "Hi, Sue!" he boomed. No one today calls me Sue. I stared, with a feeling I was beginning to recognize of being caught. "Don't you know who I am?" he asked, looking a little disappointed. "I'm Harley Schwartz." Harley? This stolid man with jowls? Harley, loud, irrepressible, light on his feet, who was first over the fence to grab the goalposts? Harley, who had jeered at me in the halls? Had I ever thought I'd see Harley again? Had I ever wanted to? I tried to subtract twenty-five years from him, adding hair, taking away flesh. As if I'd been turning a lens, within moments Harley came into focus. "Harley! No kidding!" I exclaimed. I didn't have much else to say.

Later that night I peered in my mirror. Meeting Harley had been like walking up to a magical glass in which I glanced at my reflection, looked away for what felt like moments, and then saw a stranger, twenty-five years older, gazing back. Harley was only one of many aftershocks. People whom I had forgotten, or who had frozen in my memory, appeared as if out of a time warp: a girl I'd played hopscotch with down the block; my ninth-grade homeroom teacher; the Ames newspaper editor I'd worked for when I was sixteen; my college Big Sister, who had helped me to adjust to campus life as a freshman; a fellow survivor of Old English in graduate school. Hearing from them was like attending an ongoing reunion held at my mailbox.

Sometimes I heard from strangers who felt they *ought* to have been part of my life. They said they knew me so well it was as if we were old friends. A man in his eighties called to ask me to spend a weekend with him and his wife in their lake cottage two hundred miles away. A sixteen-year-old girl rang at midnight to tell me she just wanted to say hello. I was cordially invited to stop in and visit readers in places like Cleveland, New York, Buffalo, and Sioux Falls, South Dakota. Sometimes they weren't sure whether I was *really* like the subject of my books. One man who came to a public reading said afterward, with obvious disappointment, "You weren't what I expected." I had spoken about some of the difficulties in my life, and I think, like Brian, he'd wanted me to be certifiably "happy." Another man called me up, said he'd read four chapters of my first book, thought we had a lot in common, and asked me for a date. He finished the book, and we have now been married — happily — for two years.

As I coped with responses to my memoirs, I often wavered between who I am now and who I was then. The present kept melting into the past. A girlfriend I had alternately loved and hated in sixth grade, who had soon afterward moved away, wrote me a chatty, reminiscent letter. Having recognized herself in my book,

167

she was curious about what had happened to some other former sixth-graders. In the same day's mail I heard from a woman who had been a sophisticated college senior when I was a gawky freshman and who, I'd erroneously thought, had been totally unaware of my existence. Her note included a description of how she remembered me, an eerie refraction of my own memory. Holding both the sixth-grader and the college senior in my mind at once, while transposing them into their forties, was a feat that I wished F. Scott Fitzgerald had been there to witness, noting my mind's ability to hold two opposing ideas at the same time and still function. At such times my life seemed like a collapsed kaleidoscope, colored fragments changing into patterns that in turn blurred into one another.

Meetings with or letters from old friends and acquaintances also reminded me how differently we had mattered to each other. All my former teachers were emblazoned on my memory, many with dramatic intensity. In my college memoir, I wrote about a professor, Mr. Abernathy, who had steered me toward the field of American literature, and whose tweed-jacketed, pipe-smoking, tennis-playing self I had silently adored. Many of his former students remarked on the accuracy of my fondly ironic portrait; one friend of his had me inscribe a copy of my book for Mr. Abernathy as a gift. But I never heard a word from the man himself. While I grudgingly admired his disinterest or self-restraint, I also realized that although Mr. Abernathy had influenced my life, he had probably not even remembered me.

Another professor whom I'd mentioned only briefly wrote me several long letters. Though many years retired, he not only remembered me affectionately but reminded me of a brief visit I'd had with him and his wife in London one summer. I had pictured him as aloof and more devoted to books than to students; yet his letters showed concern lest I might have found him cold during an academic crisis in my life when, he sadly told me, he instead "felt helpless about knowing what words to use to console and comfort." If I had not realized how little Mr. Abernathy noticed me, I had failed to appreciate how I'd been valued by Mr. Slater.

Some readers wrote me to explain or repair frayed threads to our mutual past. A college creative-writing teacher who had not realized how much to heart I had taken his acute criticisms enlightened me, gently, about *his* stresses during that year in the 1950s: his contract had been terminated, his wife was pregnant, he was filled with anxiety about where to go and how to support his family. If he had been harsh, he told me, it had been unintentional. He was sorry. I was sorry, too, for having caused him belated pangs; for my own young hypersensitivity; and for my unavoidable ignorance about the difficulties of life that cause unintentional harshness.

Some of the long-distance reconciliations were subtle and moving. My most important high-school boyfriend had never gotten in touch with me since I'd left for college. Now he wrote me, hesitatingly, from the hometown he'd never left. I had hoped he could hear the tenderness with which I had written about our time together. His short letter, straightforward and a little awkward, reassured me. Referring to an anecdote about my mother's flicking the porch light to get me to come in from his parked car, he mentioned his own teenage daughter and said, "The porch-light routine is still being used in Ames — this time at our house. It hardly seems possible." In his words I heard an echo of my own amazed awareness of the passage of time.

Another boyfriend, this one from college, not only wrote but even called and took me to lunch on a recent visit to Minneapolis. I had mused in print about why he and I had never managed to establish any emotional intimacy — let alone an easy good-night kiss. Now Dugal told me: he'd been as scared as I, just as unsure of his own sexual attractiveness. I left that lunch knowing something had been satisfactorily explained to the timid, self-critical girl I had been. She now knew she had not made some dumb mistake, that nothing probably could have brought her and Dugal together then. Looking at Dugal now, intelligent and delightful, I also told myself that my judgment of character in men had been at least occasionally sound.

Some readers wanted to assuage some of the pain in my past. They gratefully acknowledged the importance of seemingly small losses in childhood, which they had suffered too. Sometimes they sent gifts. One woman, reading how I'd failed to win an award for selling Camp Fire Girls candy, enclosed her own thirty-year-old but still gilt-edged Order of the Bon-Bon Certificate. Referring to my consternation as an eighth-grade leaf collector who didn't know what a gingko looked like, three women — one in Texas, one in Missouri, and one in Iowa — sent pressed gingko leaves "so you will finally have one." Some gifts were less tangible. Our high-school homecoming queen, whose tranquil loveliness I'd envied, wrote me that she, too, had felt insecure in her swimsuit because she thought her stomach stuck out. Impossible! I thought to myself, but I was still pleased she'd told me.

What struck me most about the several hundred letters I eventually received was the hunger of "ordinary" people to have their lives recorded and valued. In long letters filled with bits of their own biographies, readers said again and again, with wistful and belated recognition, "You've told *my* story."

I could also sometimes hear surprised delight that someone had thought our lives were worth writing about.

A former Ames boy, now a Las Vegas lawyer, wrote briefly but poignantly: "Not so long from now no one will remember playing kick the can in Tom Brayton's back yard. John Murray will never again carom a long fly ball off the side of the boys' locker room at Welch, and no one will remember Jim Dresser's jump shot from the right of the key in the seventh overtime. But it was important then, and it is very important now. Thank you, Sue." I had not remembered the fly ball or jump shot, but I was glad the lawyer had.

Gifted with memory and anecdote, these readers often made me wish they'd write their own memoirs. Since I had mentioned clearing tables at the Union Grill in Ames, one woman wrote, "I too cleared tables there. Our uniforms were then green and we had a small pocket over our left breast which we saved for seldom-received tips. This pocket became known as our 'Tit Pocket.' " Another confessed: "I, too, bought *Photoplay* and *Modern Screen*, pasted Robert Wagner (and Tab Hunter and Rock Hudson) on my bedroom wall and spent evenings playing solitaire, promising myself that if I won without cheating, that meant that someday I'd actually meet Rock Hudson. Holy Cow. I've never admitted that to anyone before, but I'm sure you'll understand." Some were hauntingly frank: "On finishing your book, I suddenly found myself in 1982 — disarmed. You telescoped my life in a way that left me torn. Was there anything in my early life that prepared me for the devastation I have experienced in the last twenty years? I think so, but right now I'm having trouble sorting that out."

The importance of feeling remembered — of having one's everyday life, pleasures, and sorrows set down in the semipermanence of print — came home to me poignantly at another book-signing gathering. My former high-school drama coach, whom I had respected and loved, appeared with an urgent question. I had written about the death of his small daughter and its effect on me twenty-three years before. I had changed names and a few identifying facts, as I did with anyone easily recognizable. Although her real name was Susie — like mine, so I had never forgotten it — I had called her Mary. After grasping my hand, and congratulating me on my book, he paused. Looking intently into my eyes, his face strained and shadowed by that old and terrible loss, he said, "I have to know one thing. You called her Mary in the book. Did you remember her real name?" I assured him I had, and his face eased.

Not all my audience was convinced that I *did* remember my facts correctly. "Weren't you making up the 'Mystery Farm of the Week'?" more than one person at public readings asked me suspiciously, referring to a popular newspaper feature I'd mentioned. Often those who had grown up in small towns, with the confidence of having detasseled corn or cheered at a high-school basketball tournament, rose indignantly to my defense on this and other matters. Young people — meaning those under forty — often could not believe the innocence I claimed for those of us who grew up in the 1950s in that Iowa town or a little later in Northampton, Massachusetts. "Could *anyone* have been that naive?" they asked. I could only attest that I had told the truth as scrupulously as I could.

But my pride at recalling details was shaken soon after my first book was published. In an admonishing phone call, an old friend, Larry, called my attention to an anecdote about *The Barefoot Contessa,* a movie whose sexual innuendo discomfited both a girlfriend and myself. I wrote about an embarrassing scene in the theater, the sniggering voices of the boys in the row behind us, Kathy's whisper in my ear. But Larry, now a sedate banker as convinced of his own integrity as I am of mine, said reproachfully, "Sue, you weren't even there! I *told* you about it! Joe's comment, Kathy's question, all of it!" Neither of us could convince the other. *Was* I there with Larry, Joe, and Kathy? Or did I see it with someone else? I can hear Kathy's whisper as acutely today as I think I did then. But perhaps because the incident was so *right*, capturing so precisely my own uneasy sexual ignorance, I seized that memory for my own. Writers cannibalize, and I'm a member of the tribe.

Ever since Larry tried to shine the light of truth into that movie-land darkness, I have thought about the "truth" of memoirs. An agent who turned down my first manuscript told me, "Go home and read Lillian Hellman. Maybe you can see how it's done." Her comment was not helpful. I had read and immensely admired Hellman's memoirs, but I knew that our stories were very different. I did not even consider then whether hers were true. Now, aware of how one clings to memories with the force of fact, I read Hellman with a more complex appreciation.

I don't think Hellman would have much liked my own stories of childhood; she would have been more interested in Angelica's. Angelica grew up in Ames a few years behind me, and when I saw her again, after the Ames memoir appeared, she was an accomplished artist. Angelica told me, with long-held anger, how she had reacted to my book. "I sometimes wondered when I was in high school what kind of life the rest of you led," she said. "Now I know. I didn't experience any of it."

The daughter of a Sicilian immigrant, Angelica had lived in a tiny run-down section of Ames beyond the railroad tracks, known satirically as Little Hollywood. Her father had been a janitor at an elementary school. She had had to work as a waitress — illegally, since she was underage — after school every afternoon and evening. She had never attended any of the parties and dances I had written about. Her mother had sewn in a local industry Ames prided itself on; it was a sweatshop, Angelica told me, so hot in summer that at regular intervals, all the women were forced to stand up and take salt pills from the manager's hand.

Dating? Angelica laughed bitterly. She had not been permitted to go out with any American boys, since her father had hoped she would marry someone at home in Sicily. What she knew of Ames boys wasn't encouraging. She remembered the pretty young daughter of one of the sweatshop workers; this shy girl used to meet her mother every night after work to walk her home. One evening the girl was not there. After that she appeared once, blank-eyed and stony-faced, and then was whisked out of town to a far-off aunt. She had been gang-raped, Angelica said, by some high-school boys who'd been on a toot in Little Hollywood. Angelica named some names. I knew them: popular kids whose families were well known and respected. Angelica's Ames was clearly not my quiet, middle-class, self-satisfied town.

After talking with Angelica, I have become even more sensitive to the shadings, perspectives, and interpretations with which different people see a shared past. All the voices from Brian Beeman's to Angelica's have made me consider other ways I might have written my two memoirs. Was life really like that? Did I tell the truth? Did the way I now feel about the past mean I'd felt the same way then? The kaleidoscope keeps turning. It can make me dizzy. Then I have to stop, put it down, take a deep breath, and determinedly look out the window into my present. There I can stay, trying not to decide whether I'm happy, until the phone rings and someone else says, enigmatically, "This is a voice out of your past!"

# Up with "Domestic"!

I CLUTCHED my bubbly water, nibbled on carrot sticks, sneaked powdered-sugar rum balls at discreet intervals, and tried to hold up one side of a literary discussion. It was one of those tinselly holiday parties too large for everyone to sit down, small enough so guests tried to make conversation, and attended by people who vaguely knew each other but who moved around determinedly. In my little group, several women and a man were discussing favorite writers, and one woman said, "You absolutely *must* start reading Francine Prose." "Is she one of those domestic writers?" the man asked with wariness and a touch of disdain. "What do you mean by 'domestic'?" I piped up in sudden irritation, almost choking on my rum ball. He looked uncomfortable. "Well, *you* know," he said.

I snorted, and the woman talking about Francine Prose hurriedly went on. In fact, I did know what he meant, though the values he and I placed on the word were undoubtedly different. Not long ago a New York editor sent me back a manuscript, explaining that she found it "too domestic" and "not political enough." "When you get really angry," she added, "let me know. That's what we're interested in." I snorted then too.

An odd word, "domestic." For such a modest adjective, it is an emotional chameleon. When used to modify the products and politics of men, it has a virtuous air: "domestic manufactures," for instance, describes industries that need patriotic protection from foreign imports. A president's "domestic policy" is scrutinized by commentators as seriously as his foreign policy, and when he is reported "closeted with his advisers on his domestic program," no one thinks he is demeaning himself.

But when applied to the works of women, "domestic" undergoes a change. It becomes dull and shabby. Women have "domestic duties," connoting brooms, dust rags, and dishpans. A woman who says "I lead a rather domestic life" knows she is admitting a culpable lack of involvement in larger and more important issues. Guiltiest of all are women artists who "confine themselves to domestic subjects," meaning household scenes and family affairs that have limited interest. A male artist, on the other hand, can deal with domestic subjects in an ennobling way. Think of Van Eyck's Arnolfini and his bride, Redon's flowers, Hopper's interiors. And who has ever accused Vermeer of being trivial?

Women writers have been alternately praised and criticized for being "domestic." In late-nineteenth-century America, for example, when women like Rose Terry Cooke, Alice Brown, Mary Wilkins Freeman, and Sarah Orne Jewett wrote many of the popular short stories we now label "local color," most critics approved of their homely subjects, their attention to authentic detail, and their dramatic flair. After all, Emerson, seeking the spiritual in the intimate world around him, had argued, "What would we know the meaning of? The firkin in the fire, the milk in the pan." But few male critics believed these women writers belonged in the important mainstream of literary tradition.

Some twenty years ago, as feminism gathered fresh energy, women writers were again lauded for introducing new subjects into literature: man as an unsatisfactory domestic animal; female sexual experience, including pregnancy and childbirth; the complexities of female friendship; women loving women. One woman said to me after reading Margaret Drabble's *The Millstone,* "Until now, no one ever described how I felt about having my baby." My female college students, introduced to Doris Lessing's *The Golden Notebook,* were sometimes interested less in its politics than in her matter-of-fact discussion of orgasms and menstrual periods; they couldn't believe someone was actually writing about such intimate feminine detail. An older student, recently divorced, reported about Sue Kaufman's *Diary of a Mad Housewife,* "When I came to the part about the fancy Thanksgiving dinner that no one would eat, it brought back such memories I began to cry."

But today critics are again impatient with women who write about the "purely personal." The implications and contradictions in that phrase are fascinating. Is its opposite "impurely personal"? Should we hope for writing that is "purely impersonal"? Or, to indicate greater richness, "impurely impersonal"? *Can* a story be impersonal or abstract and still compel interest, or is human character — individual, rather than general — essential?

What does "personal" mean, anyway? Is it, like "domestic," a word that changes tone with its sex? A male public figure resigns for unspecified "personal reasons," and observers sympathetically speculate about illness, family trouble, or financial problems. A man who has "a personal touch" is gifted with tenderness, intuition, or unusual communicative skills. But a woman novelist who writes a "purely personal" story is diminished, her tale a minor one, her interests probably dismissed as "domestic."

I have always felt that a powerful narrative depends on whether a reader can sense a bond between him/ herself and the human characters in the story. That bond depends on closely observed personal detail that the reader can recognize, on feelings the reader can understand, on experiences he/she can share. I intently follow *Anna Karenina* not merely for its "ideas," its social or political sweep, but because Tolstoy makes me care about what happens to Anna, Vronsky, Kitty, Levin, and Karenin.

This kind of caring — identifying with a particular human being or beings — does lead to political and social concern. Women Against Military Madness, a remarkable peace organization, surely was formed partly because women were able to imagine war in individual, personal, and domestic terms: *their* children killing or being killed, the suffering of other children and other mothers in other countries. The "other" becomes oneself. We shudder at the impersonality of military rhetoric — "terminating with extreme prejudice," "body count," "acceptable losses," "Star Wars" — because we know that these terms have forgotten the individual, the human, the domestic. Mothers Against Drunk Driving began with an individual mother whose child was murdered by a drunk driver. Who would have responded as intensely to a chart of statistics? To an abstract study? To something that wasn't "purely personal"?

But literature does not have to chart that leap from individual case to social action. Whoever tells us about a specific human being in fresh and memorable language enlarges our sympathy and understanding. Someone who reads Joan Didion's personal essay "In Bed" learns not just about Didion's migraines but also about the devastating effects of chronic illness, the self-flagellation of those who suffer, the need to endure and even grow in the face of pain. With good writers, detail becomes luminous, so that, in an Emersonian sense, spirit shines through.

The woman who wept at Sue Kaufman went on to

change her life — not, of course, because of one novel, but because she gradually realized that the conditions in which she lived were intolerable. The literature she read had, as we used to say, "raised her consciousness," a cliché with the underlying activist and communal sense of "raising the roof." It had done so by being both personal and domestic.

So I lean toward, not away from, novels or memoirs that are authentically domestic, telling important truths about home and household, daily life, and family affairs. Of course such writing can be boring; so can writing we call political, social, or historical; experimental or technically brilliant. But the best domestic writers, firmly and convincingly grounded in detail, lift me up, raise the roof, and triumphantly carry me beyond their walls into the wider membership of the *human* family.

# SEVEN

# Coming Home

# Alarms

NOW I HAVE A NOTE taped to my window alarm: "WATCH OUT," it says, in bold black letters. I've taped it on the inside, because it's a warning for me, not for burglars. Yesterday morning, dazed with sleep and a dull headache, I stumbled downstairs into my stuffy dining room and jerked the window up for some fresh air. Suddenly something seemed to explode in front of me, a high-pitched whistle so piercing I felt it tear through me like shrapnel. After a few moments I realized what it was: the dying blast of the carbon dioxide cartridge on my window alarm. All I could do was wait until it was over and hope my neighbors hadn't called the police. They hadn't. No one was listening. My daughter, Jennifer, huddled behind me long after the alarm had ceased. I wondered if my ears had been permanently damaged. While I mixed the Malt-O-Meal for breakfast, my hand wouldn't stop trembling.

Jennifer doesn't like the window alarm, because she knows she's not supposed to set it off, but she loves our Securitee Burglar Alarm. It's a small box whose ultra-sonic beams cover a cone-shaped area at the base of our stairs, so if someone comes creeping past it, it will emit a loud buzz. It only sounds nine seconds after the alarm is tripped, however, so I gloomily figure an intruder has

183

enough time to get to the top of the stairs. What will he do then? Head for one of our bedrooms? Shoot? Or — I hope — turn and run downstairs and outside? I haven't gone into any of these scenarios with Jennifer. She thinks just having the alarm is all the protection we need. She shows it proudly to her friends, letting them trip the alarm and standing close to the box so she can shut it off before I yell at her. At night she likes to set it herself and then race up the stairs as fast as she can, as though the ultrasonic beams were chasing her. In the morning she hovers at the top of the stairs, gathering courage to make a dash into the living room to turn it off before it can "see" her. Jennifer thinks it's a game.

When Jennifer asked why we were getting all these alarms, I told her part of the truth. A house had been broken into down the street, I said, and they hadn't caught the man. That was true. I didn't tell her that a young, pretty wife lived there with two small children. That she'd started to enter the house one sunny noon, after picking up her children from nursery school, and that she'd noticed the door unlocked. That she'd called the police from a neighbor's house. That on the daybed in the study they'd found her tennis dress carefully laid out, next to a pillow, some rope, and a jar of Vaseline. "Looks like he had a real party in mind," one of the cops said. "What do you think he was planning to do with the kids?" a neighbor asked me. "Is that why he needed the Vaseline?" That was the day I went to the hardware store to buy the alarms.

Last summer some enterprising feminists in Minneapolis organized a march called "Take Back the Night." They wanted other women, angry at having to fear for their safety on city streets, to join one Saturday night in a rally at a city park that has been the scene of recent rapes, muggings, and murder. Then we'd all march a mile down Hennepin Avenue, a sleazy street in the heart of downtown where the city fathers have not yet cleared the porno houses, the prostitutes, the pimps and drunks. I wanted to go. Yes, I am angry that I cannot walk around my quiet neighborhood at dusk without watching to see who is walking ahead of me, behind me, or passing me in a slow-moving car. But I couldn't find a friend to go with me to the rally, and I knew that if I parked my car near Loring Park and then marched downtown, I might find myself having to walk alone back down Hennepin Avenue late on Saturday night. I couldn't take that chance. I stayed home.

A week or so after the march, I was chatting on the phone to a close friend. I've always envied her home, bordering as it does on Lake of the Isles, a Minneapolis lake with real ducks and geese, as well as joggers, cross-country skiers, and ice skaters. The neighborhood has some of the most inviting older homes in the city, stone mansions, fake Tudor stucco manors, and brick colonials. It seems to emanate security, safety, country living in the midst of a city. My friend was shaken that morning, though; her own perimeters had been breached. It had just happened, she said, to a friend of a friend. Julie was out for an early run around Lake of the Isles, before breakfast, when no one was near to break the quiet of the morning. I knew how Julie must have felt. As my friend continued, I could imagine myself jogging next to Julie, becoming Julie, hearing the gentle lap of the waves against the low banks of the lake, listening with one part of my mind to the birds, the ducks, and the distant traffic, while with the other part I planned my day.

As I jogged along lazily, I saw another jogger approaching me. I didn't look at him closely, though I noticed he was scruffy. Unusual in this neighborhood. But it wasn't polite to stare. I continued jogging. Suddenly, somehow, we collided. Still not looking at him, I muttered an apology and hurriedly jogged away. But a few steps later a terrifying thing happened. I felt a leather belt around my throat. Then everything gets confused. He pushes me ahead of him into some bushes at a turn of the shoreline, muttering to me to keep my eyes closed or he'll tighten the belt and strangle me. Then he strikes me, hard, and I pass out. When I come to, he is inside me, pushing, cursing, hurting me. I try not to look at him. I am as still as possible. Then he is standing above me. He strikes me again and I close my eyes. When I open them again, he is gone. I manage to hobble home and my husband calls the police. But I can't identify him. . . .

"It could have been me," I said quietly to my friend when she had finished. "I go around a nearby golf course sometimes at odd times of the day. It could be me. They didn't get the man?" My friend was silent for a moment. "You know what Julie said to the police?" my friend said. "She guessed she was being misled by the mug shots they showed her. She said she realized she was looking for a kind face." "A *what*?" I said incredulously. "A kind face," my friend repeated. "She was so grateful he hadn't killed her."

That same night I was invited to a Labor Day picnic. I had been looking forward to it, since the Meridens give wonderful parties, choosing their company as carefully as their menu, so that I always leave warmed by good conversation as well as good food. Having served ourselves with tender roast pork and stuffing, ratatouille, French bread, salad, and fresh peach pie, we settled at tables on the green lawn, where pink and white petunias gleamed beneath colored lights draped in the shrubbery. Most of us were old friends. At my table were two of my favorite men, both happily married, so we flirt peacefully with each other, mutual appreciation without endangering invitation. I spoke to the scientist about life after forty, his sabbatical, his research, his return to teaching at the beginning of a new school year. He is the sort of man who can talk about the meaning of a liberal arts education without a single cliché. Then I turned to my other dinner partner, a Shakespearean scholar, and we argued companionably about the nature of realism, genres in the novel, and the current state of poetry. Eventually we all stopped talking and concentrated on dessert. The peach pie was delicious, with a flaky sweet-butter crust and just the right redolence of cinnamon. I sighed happily and drained the last of my white wine, wondering if a second glass would give me a headache. Then I heard the Shakespearean say to the scientist, "So your college didn't approve credit for R.O.T.C.?" No, I chimed in, we hadn't. We agreed our male students could take R.O.T.C. at the nearby campus where the Shakespearean teaches, but we wouldn't give them academic credit. It would violate the principles of a liberal arts education, I said with a smile toward the scientist. "I don't know," the Shakespearean said thoughtfully. "We might look at R.O.T.C. as an outlet for male violence. Let them take out their aggressions on the training ground."

My morning conversation flashed into my mind, and Julie, and her experience with violence. "Nothing will make any difference," I said with a bitterness that surprised me. "R.O.T.C. or no R.O.T.C., men will still vent their brutality against women. We will never be safe." Both men looked at me, startled. The scientist stopped eating his peach pie and put his fork down. "Oh, come on, Susan, it's not as bad as all that, is it?" he asked. "Oh yes it is," I snapped back, my voice rising. I told them about the wife down the street, and about Julie.

The woman across the table, who had stopped her own conversation to listen, said quietly, "I'm not surprised. That almost happened to me. Last New Year's Day. I was running down Summit Avenue, early too, before breakfast. I thought no one else would want to be outdoors on such a cold morning. I was layered up, sweatshirt, jacket, a scarf over my face. I must have looked like a lump. There was a man running toward me. He was heavily layered too; I couldn't see his face under his ski mask. When he passed me, he stopped dead. He grabbed me and pinned my arms against my body. I screamed, but my voice was muffled in my scarf. He just held me like that, so tight he bruised my arms inside all that clothing. Then all at once he let me go. He ran off. I ran home and called the police, told them to hurry over to Summit, he'd still be jogging. Do you know what they did? They asked me how old I was, how much I weighed, whether I was married, did I run on Summit often. They didn't go out to try to find him." I looked at her. She was someone I didn't know well, but I felt a surge of intimate feeling toward her. Then she looked down at her plate. After a moment the Shakespearean shrugged. "God," he said. "What can you do?"

I decided to get a second glass of wine. As I walked across the freshly mown lawn to the buffet table, I heard the low murmur of talk beginning again at my table. How could I have been so vehement? What was the point? Why did I sound as if I were accusing my two friends, who simply happened to be men? I poured the wine and cut another small piece of pie. This was a truly civilized evening, I thought, the kind of dinner party Virginia Woolf might have celebrated. Yet just beyond this enclosed backyard, just past this lilac hedge strung with red and blue lights, just on the other side of this quiet street, what was waiting? What might be hiding behind that large oak, what squatted in the alley? I was seized by a sadness as violent as my bitterness.

When I left the party that night, my host and I hugged each other. Tom Meriden is a kind man, warm and generous, and I love him dearly. His wife and I walked to the car, arm in arm. Then she turned to go back to the house and her other guests. It was dark in the street, a cloudy night with no moon. Before I opened the car door, I instinctively flinched and looked in the backseat.

Now I also have a Shriek Alarm. The Jaycees advertised them in our local newspaper. It is a small tube that is supposed to emit a startling noise, like my window alarm, if you press a button. Presumably it will scare an intruder, or summon a neighbor. I thought of riot-control gas, but I'm afraid I'd make a mistake and blind myself. I keep the Shriek Alarm in a Kleenex box near my bed. It doesn't make me feel much better, but it helps.

At night I sometimes lie in my bed awake and look at patterns of light on my ceiling, glare from the porch lamp next door, or a full moon refracted through my apple tree. I think of my Shriek Alarm, just an arm's reach away; the Securitee Alarm, its silent beams patroling my living room; the window alarms, their tiny metal flags poised for any upward movement. Just outside my upstairs window I can see tree branches, dark twisted lines against the sky. Some nights, especially white snowy nights, I think of us all locked in our separate houses, sheltered behind our walls, huddled in our beds for warmth against the cold. No one would want to be out on a night like this, I think. No one would be stealing across the frozen yard, testing the storm window, pushing against the dead-bolt lock. Tonight, maybe, I am safe. But still, as I close my eyes, I can see the dark tree branches, looming across my window like bars.

# Living with an Architect

"OF COURSE that toaster oven will have to go," James said casually, as he leaned against the door and surveyed my kitchen.

"It certainly won't," I snapped back. "I use it every day to make toast and heat muffins and lots of other things." I had agreed to marry an architect, James Stageberg, F.A.I.A., with thirty years' acquired tastes and convictions, and I was just beginning to learn what that meant.

"But it's so ugly!" James protested. I looked at my oven. True, the metal was no longer shiny, the glass door was coated with burned-on grease, and it was not a thing of beauty. But I had used it in my kitchen for several years, and one just like it before that. I had lived here with my daughter for more than ten years, mistress of my own house, and I was not going to give up my autonomy — or so I thought.

"Look," I said firmly. "I know you only buy appliances if they happen to be sleek, German, and in the Museum of Modern Art. I buy them if they work."

"You don't need it," James argued. He was digging in his heels too. "For toast you can use my toaster and you can heat up muffins in my oven." His toaster was sleek, German, and probably in the Museum of Modern

191

Art. My thick slices of homemade bread always got stuck in it.

"Certainly not," I said disdainfully. "I'm not going to heat up the whole kitchen in the middle of summer just to warm a muffin."

"I have central air-conditioning," James pointed out. This was a telling remark; it was one of the reasons I claimed I had agreed to marry him.

"That's not the point." I veered and tacked. "It's just too expensive to use a big oven to heat one little muffin."

"I'd rather pay the utility costs than have that ugly rusty thing in my kitchen," James said firmly. When he left that night, I was unconvinced. I didn't sleep well. How could I survive without my toaster oven? What was I getting into? What was I giving up? Whose kitchen was this going to be, anyhow? By the time dawn came, I was almost convinced that we would have to call the whole thing off. Then the phone rang.

"Good morning," James caroled cheerfully. He is far too happy in the morning. "Well, I've solved the problem. I can put a little shelf just between the oven and the wall, where nobody can really see it."

"See what?" I asked crossly. I am not happy in the morning.

"That hideous toaster oven," James replied smugly. "If it's that important to you, we'll find room for it. But maybe," he added hopefully, "when you see how it looks over here, you'll change your mind." Though I had no intention of changing my mind, I was mollified. So the engagement was still on.

The battle of the toaster oven was, in fact, only a preliminary skirmish in a long and continuing struggle. Architects are not like other husbands. Most men, other wives tell me, still cling to one part of the old-fashioned marriage contract: the woman is in charge of the house. She arranges its decoration and its furnishings, visits the decorator's studios, haunts the showrooms. Even if she brings home samples or persuades her husband to look at a sofa or carpet, she is asking for assent, not for advice. And in the end, she tells her husband where to put the sofa and hang the pictures.

Architects, on the other hand, would never dream of merely advising. Far from relinquishing control of their living spaces, they assume, naturally, that by education and training they are superbly fitted to command. Indeed, an architect surveying plans for a house often has a military air, mapping a campaign and deploying troops. If he or she happens to be a gifted designer, the results can be marvelous. I was delighted by the airy, well-lit spaces James created for my daughter and myself in an addition he designed for his house. Since I barely passed plane geometry and can never visualize anything in three dimensions, I was grateful that he could see just where windows ought to go, how to fit closets into unused corners, and even where to place my ficus tree.

But I somehow imagined that once the spaces were created, I would be in charge of the details. I was wrong. Of course, when James insisted that we choose all our major pieces of furniture together, I understood; this was, after all, our joint house. But I was surprised when I realized we also had to confer on picture frames, magazine racks, and canisters.

The day I wanted to hang a fuchsia plant, matters came to a head. It was a simple problem, I thought; the fuchsia plant on our roof deck was slung over a railing, its hook twisted at an angle. Not only did this angle crush the flowers against the wall, but the fuchsia wasn't getting enough light. Why not dangle it instead from a bracket? In my own house, I'd hung lots of plants that way.

I hurried out to the nearest hardware store. Its selection of brackets wasn't extensive, but I was able to reject a fake bronze one and another that was painted gold. I was quite proud of my acumen as I bought a black bracket, almost like wrought iron, and took it home. I laid it on the kitchen counter so that James could hang it that afternoon.

Only he didn't. "What *is* that thing?" he asked in dismay, when he arrived home for dinner. "A bracket," I said defensively, immediately realizing that I was in trouble. "You don't expect me to hang *that* anywhere, do you?" he said. I became indignant. "It's the simplest bracket I could find," I said, "and I want to give that fuchsia plant on the roof a chance in life." Patiently, James pointed out that this bracket had fanciful scrolls; if it had been completely unadorned, it might have been suitable. It was also not real wrought iron. Overall, he pointed out in conclusion, it was not very attractive.

"Brackets don't HAVE to be handsome," I shouted. "I've never SEEN a handsome bracket." Nonsense, James said encouragingly; obviously I just hadn't looked in the right places. I was sure to find the right bracket somewhere. I groaned. Since I needed to locate a bracket that was sleek, German, and in the Museum of Modern Art, my search might take years. Meanwhile I returned to the hardware store for a refund, explaining that my husband found the bracket ugly. I wondered how the salesman would record that complaint.

Next evening, when we were entertaining another architect and his wife, I asked her advice. "Oh boy, I know what you mean. I've been there," she said feelingly. "Next step is the architectural hardware catalogs. If you can find them. Actually, the best thing is to hope that maybe someday when you're in New York, you'll see something in some little shop on Madison Avenue. But I think you ought to give up on the fuchsia and get a potted begonia instead."

If I'd noticed the unnecessary curves on that bracket,

I could have saved myself some trouble. I had early learned from James that form should follow function. And I should have known better about the phony wrought-iron finish. Phony was unforgivable. I rather liked that touch of moral rigor. It had an idealistic purity. I had seen that quality on our second date. James had craftily invited me to have a drink at his house before going out to dinner, and when I walked through his soaring entrance hall, I could see why. He was a good architect. Glancing around the main floor in admiration, I saw a gleaming oak table with a vase filled with dewy daffodils, a bright yellow note of cheer on this cold, snowy winter afternoon. But they looked too fresh to be real; after all, this was January in Minnesota. Nobody could find live daffodils. My heart sank. I am a snob too; I hate artificial flowers. I had recently become a convert to natural this and natural that, and I associated silk daffodils with fussy matrons who covered their wood floors with beige sculptured wall-to-wall carpeting. How could I respect a man who had artificial flowers on his table? I had liked him so much, and his house was so enchanting. But now it was all over. Dispirited, I slouched to the table and said, "How can you stand to have phony flowers around?" (I had also recently become Refreshingly Frank, or, as my daughter puts it, Embarrassing.)

James smiled but said nothing. Close up, the daffodils looked even less real. I reached out and plucked one out of its vase. Astonished, I realized that its stem was dripping. My fingers were wet. Real water. James smiled again. "I always make it a point to have some fresh flowers around," he said. I fell in love with him on the spot.

So I should have known about the phony finish on the bracket. But I hadn't sorted out the criteria for phoniness yet. I had been confused by the penguin. Just before James and I got married, I had been walking with

195

my daughter past a gift-store window, mainly filled with junk. But in the corner I saw something that made me press my nose to the glass. It was a wooden cutout of a penguin, life-size, painted in spiffy black and white and holding out, like a smug butler, a small white tray just large enough for a cup of tea. It was unexpected and charming, and I wanted it.

"Tell James to buy me this penguin for Christmas," I directed Jennifer. "Are you kidding?" she asked incredulously. By this time she had gotten to know him well too. I sighed and walked on. Jennifer was right; a phony penguin would never fit into our modern environment. I forgot about my short-lived passion until Christmas morning, when James, beaming, unearthed the penguin from the hall closet. He liked it, he told me; it was so frankly fake that it qualified as real.

So phony fake was out, frankly fake could be in. Between these parameters was a gray area, which I would only learn about when I brought home the wrong accessory, or telephone, or bedspread. The telephone looked fine to me, exactly like the one James had had on the wall, except push-button instead of dial. It *was* a little thicker, a touch heavier, with more of a base, but who cared about that? It was an older model, and cheap. James cared, that's who. One look was enough. "It doesn't *look* like a telephone," he said decisively. "It looks like an orthopedic shoe." When I returned the phone, that's what I said to the salesman.

The bedspread problem was a bit nastier. All summer I had researched bedspreads, when I might well have been doing something more productive. I had finally found an acceptable color and material, but the made-to-order spread would have to be quilted for heft and drapability. Without much thought, as he complained later, James let me pick the quilting pattern, a tidy diamond shape. When the spreads arrived, he was appalled. "No," he said. "Yes," I said ominously; "these spreads cost enough to take us to New York, and last week you told me not to buy lobster because it was too expensive." "No," James shook his head sadly, "I can't have those spreads in our bedroom." "And why not?" I asked, realizing too late that I was giving ground. "They look," he said with a finality I had come to realize was impenetrable, "like chenille bathrobes."

But if James has won several of these small battles, I am sure he often feels he may have lost the war. Whenever he walks into our study, or carries groceries down to the basement — *he* calls it the lower level — he has to face a major fact of our marriage. I store things. I file *National Geographic*s, I save my daughter's first-grade drawings and my college notebooks, and I buy extras of everything from fear we might some desperate day find ourselves out of tinfoil, tuna fish, or toilet paper.

Worse, I also refuse to hide some of my collections: I want immediate access to books, magazines, stationery, tape, paper clips, recipes, records, pencils, perfume. Any modern architect hates clutter, and James is more passionate than most. So we have had to negotiate each visible container, stack, or tray of miscellany with the skill and tact of summit politicians.

When he was designing our study, James promised I could do what I wanted with it. "This will be the one room where I promise I won't interfere," he said innocently. "Just tell me what you need, and put anything where you like." Gesturing eloquently toward piles of books waiting for a new home, I asked for shelves, shelves, and more shelves. James delivered magnificently. In his remodeled bedroom, now a study, he found a perfect place for my desk and word processor, under a window overlooking a nearby lake. He put his own desk against a blank wall. Then he filled the opposite wall with handsome oak shelving. He even magically turned what had been a plant niche into a step-up book nook, lined with yet more shelves. On the floor we put a handsome Oriental rug, rich with reds and blues. What he envisioned, I know, was something like an English library. Elegant rows of books, gilt bindings, an aura of quiet. Understated but impressive.

What I had in mind was something else entirely. After shelving all my books, most of them floppy and dog-eared paperbacks, I had lots of space left. Just what I'd wanted. Carrying home from Target heaps of clear plastic boxes, as well as some plastic-covered wire undershelf baskets, I began to lay out my supplies. One basket for tape and shipping labels; one for old snapshots; another for maps. Between baskets I happily fitted boxes of envelopes, a layer of computing magazines, cartons of rough-draft manuscripts. On my desk I had room for not only my word processor, but a letter box, a computer disk file, a bowl of paper clips, a flowered glass paperweight, and neat little piles of correspondence and miscellany. Surveying my domain, I could see that everything I would need was there at my fingertips, ready for instant use. I loved it.

James found it painful. Clear plastic boxes were uglier to him than orthopedic-shoe telephones or fake wrought-iron brackets. The day I finished moving into the study, he came and stood silently on the Oriental rug for a while. Then, looking gloomily over the shelves, he wondered aloud if perhaps he should have a cabinetmaker fit doors over everything to hide the mess. No, I reminded him, this was just the way I wanted it, and besides, it wasn't a mess. It was highly organized. I pointed out the pile of typing paper next to the stack of yellow pads next to the row of computer manuals. He kept staring at the plastic boxes. I reminded him of his promise. "I don't suppose you'd like me to put a new filing cabinet somewhere, so you could get rid of some of this stuff?" he asked hopelessly. I remembered our conversation about bedspreads. "No," I said, firmly but gently. "This is perfect the way it is."

I knew James had never seen any clear plastic boxes in an English library. A few days later I relented and removed everything from the one shelf that is visible from the door. Remembering the daffodils, I put a green plant there instead. James doesn't come in often; I find he tends to work now on the dining room table.

The process of adjustment continues. Three times I've rescued from the garbage can the cracked plastic dustcover for my hi-fi turntable. Although James feels it is hideous, I find it useful. When it reappears, he says nothing, and neither do I. After all, we love each other. Quietly I've filled the kitchen cabinets with turntables and little plastic shelves. Equally quietly James carries some of my pots and pans down to the basement (or lower level, take your choice) and hides them in the laundry room. Sometimes we find ingenious compromises. When summer faded, we decided we would use comforters on our beds, rather than the new bedspreads; we are both pleased with the way the comforters look. Next summer, we will reopen negotiations.

But I know I will never be the same again. My point of view has been irrevocably altered, and my attitude toward my environment has been sensitized. I have become addicted to light, airy space, fresh flowers, and real wood. I too distinguish between the frankly fake and the phony. I notice things.

Not long ago, I met an old friend for lunch downtown. We thought we might try a new Chinese restaurant. But when we walked in the door, I took one look at the decor — wood-grained plastic tables, a rubbery tree in the corner, and gilt ornaments on the fake pagoda beams — and turned to my friend. "This won't do," I said, in a definitive tone she probably didn't recognize.

"But we only have an hour!" she protested. "What's wrong? We haven't even seen the menu!"

"We don't have to," I said. "Look how dark it is in here. We'd get depressed. Let's walk down the block to Ginty's."

"Ginty's?" she repeated, puzzled. "But that's even worse. I mean, it's just an old diner with a counter and plastic stools."

"I know," I said patiently. "But it's authentic. Remember the wood floors? Come on, I'll explain everything as we walk. It all comes from living with an architect."

# A Traveler Returns

ON A SUNNY MORNING in Rome, lying sleepily in bed, I think about how pleasant it will be to sip hot coffee on the hotel rooftop. But, turning over on my lumpy pillow, I am also thinking about my life back home. How nice to have fresh orange juice once more, scrambled eggs, and muffins. As I picture myself falling asleep to the sound of early crickets, I hear the increasing roar of Roman motor scooters and realize I am ready to go home.

No one ever prepares travelers for returning home, its difficulties and possibilities. Somewhere on a vacation, usually toward the end, I begin to see my life at home in new ways. What I have taken for granted now appears questionable, even suspect. During my single years, I seized travel opportunities to reevaluate current entanglements, often temporarily sure, while hundreds or thousands of miles away, that immediately upon return I would be able to cut Gordian knots. Now, as I relish the holiday pleasures of my husband's companionship, I make different resolutions of change. How could I have forgotten the fun of a fierce game of gin rummy after dinner? The languorous delights of an afternoon nap? I wonder why we haven't made more time for ourselves part of our routine.

Other relationships stand out in relief, as if I could

look down from the airplane window and see below all the people in my life, frozen in time while I pass above. Sending postcards in strange cities, I think of my friends. How long has it been since I've seen Emily? Or had lunch with Marcia? I have neglected them, I now realize, and I am determined to do better.

I think of my own neglected self as well. On an early morning walk alone, falling into the thoughtful rhythm of a steady stride, I am astonished that I do not do this regularly during the week. Why can't I find quiet spaces to listen to this inner voice? And why do I have to wait for vacations in order to submerge myself in solitary pleasures? When did I last really enjoy the flicker of afternoon sunlight on a shaded path? Or read a book in two sittings? Suddenly time appears available, elastic, almost infinite.

Change seems easy as I lie in bed in an Italian hotel, waiting for breakfast and thinking about my life. Everything is miraculously clear, I tell myself, nodding confidently, and as soon as I get home, I will act on my new certainties.

Then, of course, I get home. Dazed from a long flight or drive, jostled by crowds at the airport or deafened by the roar of freeway traffic, I arrive at my front door. Almost immediately the phone rings. I had forgotten about the telephone. The St. Cloud Lutheran Women's Club inquires politely if I can speak at their fall meeting. Judy from Dayton's wonders if we need more detergent from their summer sale. My tax accountant says no, I didn't send quite enough data, and we will have to meet immediately to finish my late return.

As soon as I let my friends know that I am back, I am immersed in the intensity of other lives. We all lead lives like not very well plotted soap operas. I need to catch up on the installments I have lost, and of course I need to summarize mine.

Then I confront the mail. As soon as I open my front door, I dive for the mail. In my first hurried sorting, I look for first-class postage, letters from old friends, readers, an agent or editor. The rest, a huge heap of dross from which I have already extracted the gold, I divide into small piles on the dining room table, trying to stave off the panic that I feel as I face the accumulated evidence of all my duties and responsibilities. Bills in one tottering pyramid. How could I have forgotten to pay my Visa last month? I try not to think of all the meals, trinkets, and splurges that, in the carefree spirit of vacation, I have just added to it. The others, too, I had forgotten: Northern States Power, Jenny's school tuition, two expiring subscriptions, Dayton's (no, I'd better not order that detergent). What a complicated web it seems, the trivia of my life, as it lies in a stack of white envelopes.

The magazines and newspapers. I usually toss the papers into a corner, only vaguely regretting that I have missed the latest movie reviews, a whole sequence in "Doonesbury" and "Judge Parker," and a few deaths of celebrities I will notice, startled, in some reference a year from now. I am rather pleased to have escaped for weeks from global news only to find that the world is somehow still intact. But I am depressed by the magazines. I will never be able to read them all. Even in ordinary times, I can't keep up with the *New Yorker,* and now it seems to have spawned unconscionably in my absence, breathlessly current and alarmingly thorough. I arrange the *New Yorker*s on the coffee table in the living room, next to unread *National Geographic*s.

Moving away from the dining room table and its stacks of mail, I start the laundry, put away the dishes, and flick a few dead flies from the kitchen windowsill. Whenever I come home from a trip, the house somehow seems messier, less organized, and shabbier. The windowsill is still streaked where the last spring storm blew in bursts of dirty water. I haven't cleaned the blinds for a year, which is why they look so dusty, and I never painted those scraped spots on the wall when I moved my posters. My only comfort is that after a few days, I know I won't see it all so clearly anymore.

Upstairs I begin to unpack. I don't like unpacking. When I prepare for a trip, I enjoy the process of narrowing my choices, honing my life to whatever will fit in a suitcase, neatly folding and tucking and making everything fit. But when I unpack, I am disheartened. Everything is used and disordered, and besides, I'm not sure I like my clothes anymore. After two weeks, I don't think I'll ever want to wear that black skirt again. Even my new purchases are no longer exciting. Why on earth did I haggle for a Greek shirt? Where will I ever wear it? Does that china vase for Sarah look cheap? How did I miss the discoloration on the red Italian purse? Why did I buy all this junk anyway?

When I've gone through my mail and unpacked, I know it is time to start my daily life again. First I go to the grocery store. Just for once I don't count coupons, watch specials, or think about the cash register. Instead I load up on all my favorite treats, especially the ones I couldn't get on vacation. Cheerios. Maple-walnut yogurt. Fresh raspberries, or Haralson apples, or Florida grapefruit, depending on the season. Salt-free taco chips, frozen tofu dessert, watercress. I cheer up with each package that I tuck away into its proper corner of shelf or refrigerator.

Then, groceries safely stowed, I take a long walk. I am reassured to tick off familiar landmarks, especially ones so mundane I'd forgotten them. The flowering rosebush in the yard of the corner house. The heat pouring out the door of the coin laundry. Kids on Big

Wheels, an old man slowly pushing a clattery hand mower, the mailman who smiles at me.

While I'm walking, I calm down. I am glad to be alone again. I am delighted that my husband, whom I adore, has finally gone to work and won't be home until suppertime. Now I have a chance to remember all the resolutions I made on our trip and begin to plan more realistically. Although on my trip I'd conveniently forgotten the complexities of my life, I had also forgotten some very good things. How touched I felt yesterday when my friend Julie told me she had really missed me. How comforting to be within phone's reach, or a quick drive, of people who know and love me. How reassuring to be where I speak the language, understand what is going on around me, and handle my daily business efficiently. Back at work, I am pleased to start to prepare for new classes. After being a tourist — looking, tasting, considering, and then moving on with the determination of a honey gatherer — I am relieved to feel useful again.

As I near the end of my long walk, I circle a city lake near my house. It is so familiar to me that I do not always see it. Today I watch baby ducks swimming confidently behind their mother, and I stop to admire the sailboards, bright butterflies skimming across the blue water. The ducks and sailboards were here a few weeks ago, but I had barely noticed them. The faint cries and laughter of swimmers at the beach, the thrumming motors of cars on the parkway, and the splash of waves on the shore blend into a comforting murmur. I'm glad to be home.

# Shade in a Spring Garden

CROUCHING ON MY KNEES and mixing peat moss into the cool wet soil, I tell myself every spring that I have misspent my life. I should have planted flowers. Perhaps I might have been a landscape architect, botanical consultant, or plant-nursery owner. Instead of filling paper with words, I could have painted empty spaces with color and drenched them with fragrance. Instead of tapping at a keyboard, I could have patted seedlings into place, experimented with new varieties of peony, and dug in peat moss by the truckload. Maybe I could have made the world a more beautiful place. At the very least, I would have improved the soil with all that peat moss.

Of course, even as I wonder whether I am too old to start as an apprentice at Bachman's Nursery, selling bulbs and fertilizer, I know I'm being foolish. I'd get tired of it. I'd grow to dislike dirt, constantly chapped hands, and aching shoulders. I would probably become discouraged by plant fungus, stinging insects, and ravaging weather. While planting eighteen identical bagged and burlapped junipers, I'd think longingly of a story I wanted to write. And what would I do in Minnesota winters? To garden all year, I'd have to move to California.

I think irrationally and confusedly during the early days of spring. Moving back and forth, like a half-open tulip blown by gusty rain, I waver between idealism and facts, dream and reality. I consider not only my own life, what I've done with it so far and what I might do differently, but also the world around me. When I look at my sun-dappled garden and ponder what lies beyond its peaceful boundaries, the contrast strikes me like a cold wind. In spring I do not know what to believe: the promise of the pink bleeding heart or the facts in the morning newspaper.

One morning this April I stood in my garden, shaken to my roots, and tried to find a balance. When I had gotten out of bed, after a night of bad dreams, my heart was heavy. At breakfast, I sat with a cup of chamomile tea, poked listlessly at my shredded wheat, and started to read the paper. The front page was grim. A fifty-year-old woman was on trial for murdering her adopted three-year-old son many years ago, a crime only recently uncovered. She had abused him mercilessly from the beginning. I took in the first paragraph — beatings, starvation, genitals clipped with clothespins — and I hurriedly turned the page, looking for "Doonesbury" or Ann Landers. If I share such a story with my husband, he always scolds me, lovingly, "Why do you read that bad stuff?" I am not sure. Somehow I feel I have a responsibility to know, to acknowledge and perhaps vicariously share in some of the pain of others. But my husband is right; I don't want to be masochistic and I tend to brood. So I put the paper down, but I cannot forget.

After breakfast, I walked out the back door to my garden, a small irregular space, mostly shady. Before my marriage, I lived in a house with a large sunny backyard, where almost everything thrived. Here I succeed mainly with impatiens and begonias. Only in early spring can I really admire my garden; red tulips, white violets, yellow primroses, and rosy-fringed columbine bask in sun filtering through just-budding leaves. I wander back and forth on my path, a few winding yards of wood chips, and smile at my flowers, wishing they would stay.

On this particular morning, with that tortured boy still hovering in my mind, like a ragged picture torn from the newspaper, I stopped in front of my bleeding heart. As a lighthearted contradiction to my mood, I saw whole strings of hearts, perfectly shaped, pink with white droplets, quivering in a wisp of breeze. This was its second year in my garden. I had never gotten around to mulching it last fall, and I didn't know whether it would come up again. Yet its delicate, fairy-tale blossoms had sprung almost overnight from the long winter darkness and now arched in prodigal sprays over the sleeping flower beds. I wondered at how it had survived the deep snow, the bitter cold, its lack of covering, my neglect.

What do I make of a world like this? I asked myself. I touched one branch of the bleeding heart lightly with my finger. The branch jiggled slightly, then the tiny hearts fell back into place. I thought of the small boy, then the flowers. I took a few more steps around my tiny kingdom, noticing how many more flowers the primrose had this year, snapping and smelling a sprig of lily of the valley, before I went back indoors.

My recognition of evil, pain, and sorrow in the world and my awareness of its startling beauty clash most noticeably when I am immersed in spring planting. Spring in Minnesota is always a miracle, a transformation from white to green in what seems like a single cloudburst. On that first day, many of us, filled with sudden urgency, converge on our favorite garden centers.

The garden centers themselves are miracles. Tents have been pitched overnight, flats of flowers and vegetables set on rows of tables, bags of fertilizer and potting soil heaped like mountains, dull red clay pots stacked in the same corner as last year. Some things change, but garden centers are reassuringly the same. They disappear for months, and then one warm day, they are amazingly here again. Even though I drive by King's Greenhouse several times a week all winter, I only faintly register, without much belief, the heating lights beginning to glow behind canvas drapes sometime in February. So I am unprepared for what happens when I enter in late April.

First I see the geraniums. Filling the moist enclosed air of the greenhouse with their faint brassy odor, they spill over table after table, flaunting their gaudy pinks and corals and reds. After the black-and-white etchings of a Minnesota winter, with its subtle gray and brown tones for background, I am stunned by all this color. I try to take in the multihued sweep that beckons beyond the geraniums, striped and flecked, tiny dots and large blurs, among a forest of green leaves. Above me, hanging baskets are strung like decorations high over the tables, purple and red drops of fuchsia, pale yellow begonias, deep pink impatiens.

At the far end of the greenhouse an exit leads into the back lot. I push my cart down the aisle and emerge outside. Before me is an impressionist painting, a study in pointillist pigment, of an alpine meadow. A sea of color ripples in the morning breeze, table after table of petunias, marigolds, dahlias, snapdragons, pansies, asters, and flowers whose names and very existence I had forgotten. I slowly walk by, renewing my acquaintance. Johnny-jump-ups, lobelia, alyssum, pinks, moss rose. All are in bloom, bright heads bobbing on short stems.

A friend who runs a large nursery in Missouri once told me that annuals would grow better if they weren't forced into this early bloom, which must be snapped off at transplanting so that the flower will branch out in full luxuriance. "But people won't buy the packs if they're not showing flowers," he sighed. After a killing winter,

209

we doubting Thomas gardeners evidently need reassurance — the actual touch, smell, and color.

Wheeling between the tables, soaking in the light warmth of the April sun, I immediately forget that I came to get only one pack of impatiens, since I don't have time to transplant much today. I stop in front of each section, tempted, wanting them all. I eventually fill my cart with an entire flat — twelve packs — of Pink Blaze impatiens, as well as assorted other pots and hanging baskets I can't resist. Home, I place the plants on my front porch. I wish I could get them in the ground right now, but I am already so late to my office I must leave immediately.

The next morning I don't have to be at work until noon. As I hunt for my gardening jeans, I am almost trembling with excitement. Soon I am outdoors, my trowel in one hand and one pack of impatiens in the other. The early air is still cold, and heavy dew hangs on leaves and blades of grass. Everything seems fresh and wet, like the newness of just-born kittens. After clearing last fall's dead leaves from a small strip near the garage, I transplant one pack of Pink Blaze, then another.

I feel as if I must hurry, though I am smiling and humming repeated fragments of old songs. My sense of rush is not just because I know I must soon clean up and go indoors. I am anxious for all my flowers to begin to grow. Their roots are bound together in the plastic boxes or twisted in a ball in the single pots. They need to breathe, to move, to stretch into the earth. As I pat the soil gently around one small seedling of impatiens, with its single blossom, I look at it and imagine it filled with blooms, rounded and heavy with pink petals.

As I continue, digging a hole, separating a seedling, mixing peat moss and a little sterilized manure into the ground and then planting, scooping, firming, and tamping, I have plenty of time to think. The small boy from the morning paper returns. He seems to represent so much else I don't want to remember: the emaciated young girl crouched in the dust of a Laotian refugee camp, the welfare mother in north Minneapolis who feeds her four children donated macaroni six times a week, the homeless old man huddled inside a makeshift cardboard shelter under the icy railroad bridge. My picture of the dead little boy is from the newspaper, an old snapshot taken at his adoption; he looks normal, smiling, healthy. And before I can stop myself, I remember what was done to him to make him stop smiling.

This morning some children are playing noisily in my neighbor's backyard pool. I hear laughter, splashes, mingled shouts and happy shrieks. Pulling upright for a few moments to rest my aching back and neck, I listen. A close friend has told me that sometimes at night she hears high-pitched frantic crying from a child who lives across her alley. My friend does not know the family. The child sobs so long, so despairingly, so uncomforted, that my friend has twice gotten out of bed, put on a robe, and walked down the alley, only to stand and stare helplessly at the house. Once the father yelled in a terrible voice, "You lied to me!" Then the child cried, "Daddy! Daddy!" over and over, in the same high, frantic, sobbing voice. A next-door neighbor, discreetly questioned, said she had never noticed anything unusual. Weeks will go by when the little voice is silent, and in winter, when doors and windows are double-glazed against the cold, my friend hears nothing. The crying drifts into her bedroom only on summer nights, through the open window over her lilacs.

Perhaps I am lavishing too much care on my garden. I know that this is only the first spring morning I will spend here. If I added other mornings and afternoons, as well as several trips to King's Greenhouse, I would probably approach a forty-hour work week. All this time, for what? *"Il faut cultiver nos jardins,"* Voltaire said. When I first read that in French, I liked its emphatic sound, and even translated into English, it was still confident: "It is necessary to cultivate our gardens." But at the expense of what? I try not to add up the costs of all these flowers and supplies. Money that could go to a good cause, time spent on something only our family enjoys. I shouldn't be here, I tell myself reprovingly; I should be grading overdue papers to hand back to my class this afternoon.

I reach for another handful of peat moss. It is compacted so tightly in the large plastic bag that I have to dig it out in clumps, tearing away fistfuls at a time. I love the way it feels, feathery and crumbly, its light brown strands loosely falling through my fingers. From its label, "Pure Sphagnum Canadian Peat Moss," I dimly glimpse a far northern tundra, where once pine forests silently decayed over thousands of years. Now the forests, ferns, flowers, leaves, have ended up in this four-cubic-foot bag of peat. Since I was always more attracted to the poetry than to the facts of geology, I'm probably wrong. But peat moss does seem ancient, wrinkled and dried like the skin of the very old, but with the breath of life buried in it. When I pour water on a seedling later, the moss beneath the ground will soak and swell, holding essential moisture for the tender roots.

Then I toss some manure into the transplanting hole with the peat moss. It is black and damp, like the essence of earth, with the faintest pungent whiff of its origins. It too feels wonderful in my hands, heavy and rich. As I mix it for nutrients with peat moss, I have a satisfying sense of having done what I could to give these young plants a good start.

I wish I could do something about the dead child. He seems so real to me, as close as the fragile pink impatiens at my feet. I have a child myself, now almost grown, but

I remember her at three, her small round arms reaching up to me from her bed, warm and damp. When I held her, she nestled into me as though burrowing into the ground. I would bury my nose in her soft hair or the folds of her neck. I think of her, and I picture the dead child, once her age. I see the slaps, the beatings, the burning cigarette pushed into the pink soft skin. I hear the child's helpless screams.

Here in my garden I am not helpless. Indeed, though I gratefully give credit for the miracle of new life, I myself have an awesome sense of power. I look around at dead stalks, last fall's refuse of leaves and twigs, grayish brown remains of uprooted plants, and I know that I am about to transform these few square yards into a place of joyous color. Part of my excitement in the garden at April planting time is the instantaneous cause and effect: I plant an impatiens, a bright pink spot suddenly appears on the dark ground.

As I admire my brushstrokes, I squint at different places, different angles. I notice where I can put more plants. I am filled with hope. In my mind I am beginning to see the garden I always think I'm going to have, a magical plot inspired by childhood memories of old Mrs. Sweeney's riotous collection of hollyhocks, sweet peas, peonies, and zinnias. My ideal garden combines Mrs. Sweeney's favorites and a few fancy pages from a Wayside Gardens catalog. Of course, I can't grow any of those flowers in shade. But I look at my impatiens and begonias, and I dream. These new recruits, my brave young plants, set so firmly into peat moss and manure, will march into May, June, July, colors unfurled and banners waving.

Of course I am not being realistic. Perhaps that is why I love my garden so much in April, when it is expectant and unspoiled. I know what will happen in June. The first mosquitoes will hatch, flies multiply, other insects crawl and fly about my knees, hands, ears. Before I go into the garden, I will have to douse myself with repellent and button my shirt to the neck, and so I won't always take a daily survey. By July the midsummer heat settles on Minneapolis, sometimes a rain-soaked blanket, sometimes a thick smothering featherbed. I turn up the air-conditioning and, looking out the window at my garden, notice the weeds.

Because by July, Eden is over. The spring flowers have faded, and the lovely bleeding heart begins to turn a sickly yellowish green, drooping and dying back as if winter, even under this blazing sun, cannot be far away. Tough intrusive weeds have shouldered their way among the struggling blue flax and poppies, sinking roots underground so deeply and so tenaciously that plucked in one place, they surface again in another. When the sun glowers through a humid haze for several consecutive days, stimulating the mosquitoes to blood frenzy, I give up and stay inside.

The garden knows I have lost interest. Or perhaps some plants simply do not like their location or filtered sun. Perhaps they need more water. So they give up too. Growing lopsided and askew, they refuse to bloom, or bloom only once, with a single orange poppy, a few waves of blue flax, and then quit. Walking in the garden in late July, I tell myself I did what I could, and that's the way it is. Besides, in six more weeks, with an early frost, the growing season will be over for another year.

The trial for the dead child's adoptive mother is over too. After weeks of testimony and cross-examination, of which I tried to read merely the headlines, the jury took a scant six hours to find the mother guilty. Her lawyer, trying to make a comeback as someone with spectacular defense tactics, lost. I do not know who won. Her picture in the paper showed expressionless, beady eyes in a plump aging face, the unremarkable kind of woman who might live anywhere.

I hope I can forget the child. He haunts my garden, though I have much to be thankful for, and the world is still beautiful. At the end of summer, not all my garden is disappointing. A few purple phlox and scattered orange zinnias sparkle in late afternoon sun. On the upstairs deck and along the garage, my impatiens and begonias are so full of red, pink, and white blossoms that I plan to take some pots indoors for the winter. A sweet basil offers enough leaves for several batches of pesto, and I snip flowers from a rooftop planter full of giant marigolds.

So as I stand in my garden in early spring, I know that my efforts will not be completely wasted. Even if they were, I think I would still be here. I would continue to walk back and forth among the tulips and violets, pat the soil around my tender seedlings, and eagerly remember the flats waiting on the front porch. I would believe that perhaps this year, everything will bloom in splendor. I would certainly pause before the bleeding heart so I could marvel once again at its delicate pink-and-white hearts, dangling from the lacy branch, swaying gently in the April breeze.

# Grandmother's Story

WHEN I STOOP to slip under the cemetery chain, I feel apprehensive, as if beyond this barrier lies an old minefield. When I was a young girl, some grown-up solemnly warned me never to walk on a grave, since it was a sacrilegious affront to the body lying below. So on this hot July morning, though forty-six years old, I still zigzag carefully across the clipped grass. I head toward the back of the Iowa State Cemetery, where tall old trees shade the stones, to the knoll where my father was buried when I was seven. I stop there briefly whenever I come back to Ames.

Despite the sprawling university campus across the road, this hilltop cemetery is a quiet place. It was once alive, part of the community, a gathering place where people came and went, burying and mourning their dead. As a child, I remember other fresh graves besides my father's, newly cut flowers wilting in their vases, the soft sobbing of women at the Memorial Day services. But now the cemetery is filled: no one can be buried here who didn't buy a plot years ago. As the survivors of its occupants disappear, one by one, the cemetery is itself dying, slowly receding into the past.

As I walk through the thicket of markers, I am thinking about Lena Corum, my mother's mother, who died before I was born. My last visit to a grave was to hers.

216

I wasn't curious about her until, in mid-passage, I began to examine my own life. Then I wanted to know everything. Where do I come from? How am I like her? What can she teach me? A few months ago I saw her grave in Alexandria, Minnesota. Like my father's, her stone is simple. Lena Corum Erickson, 1874–1936. I wanted it to tell me something, but it didn't.

I have made stories of my own life, though it has not so far been unusual, marked neither by celebrity nor by any remote influence on historical events. I don't feel ordinary, but I'm not sure anyone does. "If only I could write," people often say to me; they are talking about their experiences and memories, which seem to them worth preserving. Now, in my forties, looking backward and forward, I wonder about the meaning of most lives. How many stories can I learn? How many can I tell? Lena's children do not think her life had any dramatic interest. They say she was a good woman, raised a large family, loved them all equally, suffered a long illness, died young. The end. When my mother, aunts, and uncle, all in their seventies and eighties, are gone, Lena will be gone too. I *want* her to have a story.

As I notice the names on the stones by my feet, some of them startle me. I have come back to Ames so seldom in the past twenty years that I long ago lost track of its changes. Neighbors down the block, glimpsed during trick or treat at Halloween or Christmas caroling, moved or died, and I never knew. I probably wouldn't have cared much, and indeed, I never thought about what had happened to them. But now I stop in front of a stone, already several years old: Henry Sumner, 1904–79. Mr. Sumner gone? The Sumners lived around the corner, on Forest Glen, in a big Tudor house with a funny turret. Mr. Sumner was a gentle, gray-haired man with a sweet smile. When he, rather than his wife, answered the door, he always bought *two* boxes of Camp Fire candy.

217

A few yards beyond Mr. Sumner is another newer monument, a family marker rising majestically above its modest sunken neighbors, announcing HEASTY in large letters. Underneath I see two separate names: Elbert and Elizabeth Heasty, who appeared in the same pew at Collegiate Presbyterian every Sunday when I was growing up. They were pillars of the church, as solid and unchanging as the altar and choir stalls — all of which, I now remind myself, were uprooted and turned in the opposite direction when the church remodeled its nave ten years ago. Mr. Heasty, a deacon, always led his wife down the aisle with stiff courtliness. Dressed in a dark suit with a white handkerchief neatly folded in his pocket, he had a firm chin and a military tilt to his shoulders. I thought he was the kind of father who would have looked perfect sitting at the head of a long oak dining table, carving turkey superbly. Sometimes in church Mr. Heasty nodded when the minister made a point in his sermon. Otherwise I never saw any expression on his face.

Mrs. Heasty had tight gray curls piled on top of her head, fastened with stiff tortoiseshell combs. She seldom smiled, and her glances darted sharply around the quiet church. She would turn and frown at children who were restless or noisy in the pews behind her. Elbert R. Heasty, 1901–1976. Elizabeth Jane Heasty, 1903–1980. What had Mr. Heasty been? I ask myself. Was he the treasurer of the church? Did he run the Memorial Union at the college? Or was I confusing him with Mr. Sumner?

As I stroll past other graves, stopping to study names more carefully, I try to think of what I recall about all these people who have slipped away so silently. They had been persons of importance. I can faintly hear the weighty spoken currency: "I saw Mr. Sumner downtown this morning, and he said he'd absolutely never vote for Stevenson. I didn't try to argue." "There go the Heastys, just ahead of us. Don't quarrel like that, girls, or they'll hear you."

Just behind Mr. Heasty's monument is an imposing gray-speckled column inscribed to Dean Becker, who had run the school of home economics for forty years. Dorothy Becker, 1897–1982. In life she had been a monument too, appearing on a weekly local radio program and then as a guest commentator on a women's television show. She could be seen lunching in the Union Oak Room every day, the center of a table of dignified lady professors and staff. Proud and unmarried, they were almost identical in navy crepe dresses, blued hair, and rimless glasses. Dean Becker dominated, her large bosom encased in a rigid underpinning that was always adorned with a trademark string of long pinkish pearls. At least some former students undoubtedly still remember her. But in thirty or forty years, who would?

I think again about my grandmother. An unimportant life, but soon no more forgotten than Mr. Sumner, Mr. Heasty, and Dean Becker. Whose life *is* really important? How shocked Mr. Heasty would be if he could hear my question. Surely Mr. Heasty had felt his own worth. If asked, Dean Becker would certainly have spoken up for *her* significance. Yet beyond these public selves, now so rapidly fading from memory, did they have personal stories, perhaps ones no one knew or could understand and interpret? I picture Mr. Heasty and his blank, stolid face; Dean Becker, matronly and unruffled. Mr. Heasty walking firmly down the aisle at Collegiate Presbyterian; Dean Becker, seated at the lunch table, inclining her head at someone who passes. Try as I may, I cannot imagine them at home, quarreling with wife or roommate, crying aloud in anger or waking in the morning deep in depression. Nor can I imagine them making love, laughing hilariously, or stretched out comfortably on the floor in front of a warm fire. Did either one of them sing in the shower? Dream of an old love? Wish life had been better, or longer, or shorter?

If I had known Mr. Heasty's children — I think he had two sons, much older than I, and I cannot place them — if Dean Becker had married and had children, if I could see those other Heastys and Beckers and learn what kind of people they had become . . . I pause, noticing the blinders on my imagination. I can only begin to provide personal lives for these wraiths, these vanished bodies, if I know something about their children. Why? Is that why I am so sure my grandmother has a story?

"She was a loving woman, perhaps a little nervous, a patient wife, a good mother." My aunts' misty recollections don't evoke Lena Corum for me. But my *aunts* do. They, my uncle, my mother, are all strong characters: determined, funny, ambitious for their children, energetic but also somehow resigned. I see their complications in myself, their sensitivities and fears, their anger and irony. Where did it all come from? What did they learn from Lena, and, therefore, what did I?

As I walk among the graves this morning, I realize that I am looking for connections. I do not want to see each stone as only a name with nothing behind or beyond the bare dates of birth and death. The names and dates call out for narrative shape, for meaning, interpretation — above all, for stories. I can't do anything about the Heastys or McCarthys or Beckers, but I *can* do something about my grandmother. I can try to reimagine her life, her feelings, what she wanted and what she got.

To do that, I will have to look at my own life. As I leave the cemetery, closing the gate softly, I know that in some strange way I have found a way back to Lena Corum. Perhaps, if I learn how to read it, *I* am my grandmother's story.

# Teachers

AS THE SUMMER CAREENS to a close in late August, with my daughter tugging me to Southdale, the last Sunday crowds splashing and shouting on the Lake Harriet beach, and fireworks exploding over the state fair, I finally force myself to start thinking again about school. All my life, as a student and then as a teacher, I have lived on an academic calendar. Every August I wonder about that: why I do what I do, and how long I plan to keep doing it. "What shall I do when I grow up?" has turned into "What shall I do with the rest of my life?"

Both plaintive questions have echoed in our house lately. Meanwhile, in the silent spaces, I have been trying to imagine and then listen to another voice, that of my grandmother Lena, dead before I ever knew her, whose life I have been investigating in a roundabout way. What choices did women of her era have? What did they want for themselves and their daughters? How imaginative were their dreams?

My grandmother Lena wanted her daughters to become teachers. "She taught in a country school before she married Papa," my mother remembers. "She said it was a good profession for a woman." I know so little about Lena that I treasure each nugget of information, turning it in the light to look for streaks of gold. This one tells me that although Grampa Oscar was stern and dominating, Lena was still strong enough to make teachers of all four daughters. She was ambitious for them too, insofar as a Norwegian immigrant's daughter who never lived more than twenty miles from the farm where she was born *could* be ambitious for her girls. "Nurses and teachers," my mother says without bitterness, "that's all we thought of in those days." My mother pushed a little: she insisted on attending the state university, not just the normal school.

I am a teacher too. High-school career guides outlined my alternatives in the 1950s: librarian, newspaper reporter, lab technician, fashion buyer, dietitian. College advisers suggested others: social worker, translator, editor, administrative assistant. None of these occupations seemed right for me. Frightened by science, I ignored medicine and research laboratories. Nor did I want to follow the vague plan of many classmates to simply "go to New York," to subsist on the glamour of the big city — until marriage. I chose teaching, but I pushed too: I wanted a Ph.D., high-minded students, scholarly colleagues. How could one ever tire of reading and talking about books, enjoying the intricacies and transcendence of language, sharing knowledge and ideas?

Now, after eighteen years as a college professor, I am no longer so confident. I have to delve deeper for the energy to fuel my teaching. I wonder if my lectures are growing stale. I am not sure I care about most literary criticism. I am so tired at the end of the day I cannot write. Am I burned out? If so, what next? I have never thought of doing anything else.

With an unerring sense of my vulnerability, Jennifer, my fifteen-year-old daughter, recently struck. Although she ordinarily doesn't like to converse at the dinner table, she turned one evening to my husband and myself and asked, "What should I be when I grow up?" I didn't know how to answer her. As I paused, considering, she added, unnecessarily, "I'm afraid I'll be a teacher because *you're* a teacher and *Gramma* was a teacher. I don't want to be just like you. So what else can I be?"

Today Jennifer has so many choices I didn't know where to start. Our working world is so complex, subdivided into myriad minute cells, that I momentarily imagined cities packed with high-rise office buildings, filled with highly specialized workers as a honeycomb with bees. What do they all do? I have younger friends who, variously, design jewelry, sell balloons, administer a group home, run a restaurant, and repair wicker. Jennifer giggled as I ticked them off. "Oh, sure," she said; to her these seemed unlikely occupations. Then as I cast about among women my age, the ones I know well, I came up with obvious images: editor, lawyer, varieties of teacher. I mentioned them, feebly. Jennifer wrinkled her nose. "Not old stuff like that, Mom," she said. "You used to say you wanted me to be an oceanographer."

She is right. I thought it sounded spiffy. Dreaming for my child, as parents do, of what I did not have, I pictured a career that might have kept me outside more, plunged me into that undefined region some people call the "real world," carried me to the equally mysterious "frontiers of knowledge." Also, altruistically, since her father is a scientist, I didn't want to influence her unfairly toward the arts. And I loved the ocean. "Well," I now said hesitatingly. "Actually, I'm not really sure what oceanographers do."

"Do they make much money?" asked Jennifer bluntly. Breathing deeply, I began a shaky parental lecture on the primary importance of working at something that matters. "How do you know if something matters?" she pressed. I was stymied. On my gloomier days, I am not sure anything matters. On slightly brighter ones, I think of people working in refugee camps in Cambodia, drafting child abuse legislation, sifting through cells to find a cure for cancer, organizing inner-city youth centers. Even on the sunniest mornings, when I sometimes try to weigh the relative importance of how I spend my days, I cannot always read the scales. So I go to my class and teach on faith. I think of my grandmother; she knew, without a doubt, what women should do.

My husband rescued me. "You want to love your work," he said. An architect for thirty-plus years, he is still like an excited boy at his drawing board. "Yeah, but Mom complains a lot about teaching," Jennifer pointed out. She is right; I do not tell her often enough how I still love to read and talk about George Eliot, Virginia Woolf, E. B. White — in fact, any writer I teach. I do growl loudly about erratic attendance, the occasional whiny student, stacks of blue books, long committee meetings. "Any job has its drawbacks," I said defensively. Jennifer looked distinctly uninspired.

Later that night, after Jennifer had firmly shut her door, I pondered our conversation. I felt I had somehow failed her. How simple it was for my grandmother, I thought irritably. Nursing or teaching, then marriage. No difficult choices, no midlife career crisis, no change at all. Of course, if one's husband died . . . I clearly saw the chasm looming before a widow in Grandmother's day, even in *my* mother's day, and I drew back from selective nostalgia.

With a world lying before her, what can I suggest to Jennifer? Like Lena, I am ambitious for my daughter. I think of tapping on her door and tossing her the cliché that she can grow up to be President. But I don't think I *want* her to be President, with its terrible strains and responsibilities. I do want her to reach and stretch, to be brave and bold, to push a little. How? Where? At what? I hope my vagueness indicates tolerance, a willingness to let her develop her own talents, and a recognition of how she, like me, may need to stay open to the possibility of change. As I examine my inability to answer her question, I realize I must depend on whatever lessons she has learned from me about meaning, values, and struggle. What she does with her life will partly rest on whether — despite error, faulty performance, complaining, and with sometimes faltering faith — I have been a good teacher.

# I Wish Words Would Help

🌸 MY GRANDMOTHER DIED early after a long illness, my mother says sadly. When I was in my twenties, sixty-two didn't sound young to me. But it was young enough so that I never knew Lena. I've heard so little about her life from my reticent relatives that I have a hard time picturing those last years, last months. My grandfather, reserved, gruff, and silent, was there, of course. But what about her friends? Did she have anyone she loved near her? Who did she turn to, talk to, cry with? I don't want her to have been alone.

Now that I am forty-six, sixty-two does sound too young to die. I am thinking a lot about mortality these days. My own best friend for fifteen years, who is my age, is very ill with cancer. It has recurred for the third time. She doesn't use the word "dying," and so neither do I. She has fought the malignant invaders with unfailing strength, courage, and humor; she has beaten them back twice, summoning defensive troops with formidable powers of mind and medicine. She hangs on now by a thin thread of determination, which I picture like a coil of nylon filament, almost invisible yet surprisingly strong. As the weeks pass, bringing more weakness and pain, I am afraid it may be stretched to the breaking point.

I do not know what to say to my friend. She does not

talk easily about feelings, and I do not want to embarrass her, to force tears to the surface, or to invade her privacy. I am aware that in a no-holds-barred battle with cancer, her privacy is constantly assaulted by caretakers, doctors, tests, and treatment. I do not want to take one more shred of it away.

I wish desperately there were something I could *do*. For ten years, when I was divorced and a single parent, she thought of things to do for me. When Sunday stretched before me, long and lonely, she'd call and say, "Come over tonight and have pizza on the rug with us." Some weekdays I came for lunch, while our two young daughters, born only a day apart, tugged restlessly at toys and at each other. When I talked, she listened, sympathetically and intelligently, with a loving acceptance that had been rare in my life. She knew what was important: when I bought my first house, she sent home a cutting from her French tarragon bush, so I could start my own herb garden. She met a woman at a party who she thought would be a terrific therapist for me, and she was right.

She introduced me to any single male friends she could find, and as soon as any of her husband's friends or associates became separated, she called me up to describe their peculiarities and attractions. When I became at all seriously involved with someone, I always took him to her house for approval. She and her husband invited me, singly or in a couple, to parties. Two years ago, I was married in the living room of her spacious house. We planned the wedding so it would fit in with her chemotherapy.

During all those years, I suppose I was giving her something too, but it is hard at this moment to remember what. I want to give her something *right now*, something that matters, but I can't. Other friends — she has many people who love her — vie for the privilege of bringing her lunch, or running an errand, or dropping off a new book or plant or thoughtful gift. I take my turn, not wanting to ask for more than my allotted time. She has a large and wonderful family, a husband and mother and mother-in-law, two children, all kinds of other caring relatives nearby. She does not have enough time to divide among all of us equally. Besides, in the last year, for reasons I do not fully understand, we saw less of each other than in the years before. We talked less, shared less. In the past, I would have long since pushed my way to the front of her attention and yelled, like one of our children, "Hey! Look at me! What's happening? I feel left out!" I would have asked if her illness, my marriage, our inevitably changing lives, had caused a natural separation. Or whether some unnamed grievance had caused an unnatural one. But we have no time for such discussions now. I can't raise my hand and stomp my feet. Her family needs her attention more.

Even if she *did* have more time, I do not know what I would use it to say. I am in the habit of asking her advice and often giving it back. Fifteen years ago, when we had both been home from the hospital for a day with our new babies, one of us called the other — I can't remember which — and asked worriedly, "Does *your* baby have green stuff in her diapers? I just can't stand to call my pediatrician one more time today." (Both babies did, and both mothers were relieved.) On many days we were each other's amateur doctor, nurse, comforter. When her toddler had a rash and high fever, and mine toppled off a low wall onto a concrete sidewalk, we reassured each other that everything would be okay. Through our children's tantrums, night terrors, teething, school traumas, questionable friends, puzzling behavior, infuriating back talk, and teenage testing, we said, "It'll be all right. Everything will work out. This is just a stage."

Now I want to tell my friend that everything will be

all right. I wish I had a certainty to pass on to her, not just my own fears and shaky hopes. I wish I knew, for sure, that this was just a stage, like chicken pox and homesickness. That everything would work out.

I have no advice to give her, and she doesn't want any. Except for bits of news about my life, questions about how she feels, notes on books I've read or television shows she might like, I can tell her nothing. I want to ask the source of her courage, but I do not think it is something she can pass on to me. And she has given me enough, more than I can ever put in words. I only wish words would help.

# Reunion: Coming Home

AS THE CABLE CAR CLANGED down the steep hill, I watched women sleepily opening blue or yellow doors, watering a blur of green plants behind gauzy white curtains, or basking on their steps in the soft morning sunshine. Behind me the conductor rang his bell, cables scraped harshly, and people talked loudly or shouted over their jostled shoulders. I should have been part of this happy noise and bustle, just another midwestern tourist on her way to Fisherman's Wharf. But, suddenly back in San Francisco after many years, I was instead a spectator in my own moving theater. What the city was showing me, though I hadn't asked for it, was a different version of my own life. The cable car was taking me relentlessly past pictures of who I might have been.

What if I had stayed in San Francisco after graduate school? A young woman hurried down the street, her hair rippling in the breeze, gold earrings gleaming against her tanned skin. I envied her air of purpose: she clearly knew where she was going, with a large manila envelope tucked under the arm of her crisp linen jacket. I shrugged unconsciously, as if to move beneath the heavy weight of the sheepskin coat I had left behind in Minnesota. If I hadn't married so young, I might never have left San Francisco, I thought. I too might have been living in one of these ivory Mediterranean town houses, with the cool foggy nights of San Francisco blowing through my tall-ceilinged rooms. I too could have dashed out the door at a moment's notice, striding down the street like this independent young woman. At night I might have cooked fresh seafood for a few friends, artists, and musicians — who else lived in San Francisco? — as we sampled a tender young wine someone had just brought back from the Napa Valley.

With a self-pitying shiver I remembered my last weekend, when a mid-March snowstorm buried the Twin Cities, canceling a dinner party, grounding my car. I was terrified of driving on icy roads. Would I have worried so much if I had lived all these years in a Victorian town house on Sutter or Fremont or California Street? Would I have floated more easily through life? Didn't everyone in San Francisco look more self-confident, more carefree? As the cable car clanged on, romantic mirages shimmered in front of my eyes, bright as the sunlight, gentle and soothing as the pastel doors and window boxes, enticing as the gaudy flower cart parked so casually on the last corner.

Other ghosts of who-I-might-have-been haunt other places. Some summers I drive up the coast of Maine to an island I love. As I pass through the neat, weathered-gray villages, I admire the well-kept houses, the splashes of purple lupine and white daisies in the fenced yards, the dignified small-paned windows. Everyone here has privacy, I think enviously, and a freedom to do or be what she wants. Once I passed a large white house facing the town square in one such village. It had an elegantly lettered signboard: "Wayfarers Inn. Bed and Breakfast." Could I run an inn like that? I wondered then. I saw myself cooking morning pancakes for my guests, airing the rooms, waving new friends on their way. During the day I'd walk the quiet streets, smell the salt breeze blowing in from the sea, and drift through the mists with my own thoughts.

If I had moved to Maine after my divorce many years ago, could I have settled in an inn, or found a little house by the shore? Would I have learned to chop wood and gather berries? Instead of a stuffed closet, would I own just a pair of jeans from L. L. Bean and an old hand-knitted sweater? Would I have written more and gone back to the piano? Would I have found the tranquil spirit that so often eludes me? As I listen to the Maine surf late at night, I feel a sense of returning from exile, of being at home, of wanting to stay there forever. What would I have been like if I had bent my will to that feeling fifteen years ago?

Sometimes I drive through small midwestern towns, even smaller than the one I remember from my childhood, and I wonder if I might have lived there. If I had married that earnest young man who sat behind me in Introduction to Graduate Studies, we could have ended up in a cozy college town, perhaps Mount Vernon, Ripon, St. Peter. I would have helped organize the League of Women Voters, campaigned for school-bond issues, and conscientiously read my weekly *New Yorker*. Would I have been restless? The ghost I see now cutting her flowers, filling her bird feeder, or backing her station wagon down a long drive looks at me a little wistfully as I whiz by.

Suppose I had not left Ames at all? Some girls I knew thrived right at home at Iowa State. Stay here, they advised me. Maybe you can edit the *Daily,* and you could always go on to journalism school. Pledge Theta, or be a Kappa. They get all the neat guys. You'll get to know men here, the way you never will at a women's college. . . . If I hadn't gone to Smith, would I have gotten migraines? If I had spent weekends building a homecoming float or frolicking at a sorority picnic, would I have become less intense?

This is the summer of my college reunion, and I am thinking about these questions. A few years ago, when I went back to Ames for a high-school reunion, I was wary. Most of us hadn't seen each other for twenty-five years. Many, like me, I suspect, were nervous: not, I realized with surprise as I looked around that first crowded evening, because we hadn't aged well. In fact, almost everyone looked good; we are a generation that learned about keeping fit. Women moved gracefully around the room, men wore their shirts open, and we all talked enthusiastically of jogging, skiing, or tennis. But some of us were uneasy for reasons no one mentioned. We were crowded in that hot, stuffy banquet hall not just by each other but by each other's ghosts. As we searched anxiously in an old friend's eyes for startled recognition, we could sometimes see reflected a picture of the person he or she had thought we were going to become.

Twenty-five years ago, we all had been entranced by Marilee Egerton as Juliet in the senior play. What a gifted actress she'd been, and what a future we'd all envisioned for her in Hollywood or on Broadway, with her delicate, heart-shaped face on a billboard, her name in flashing lights. I'd last heard of her at twenty-one, setting off for New York. Now, still striking with what looked like newly blond hair, Marilee flew about the room in quick, poised movements. She had been married twice, someone said, and lived now in Scarsdale with her second husband, a computer executive. They had two kids, and she didn't act anymore. When she looked in old friends' eyes, did she see the neon lights blinking, then the marquee gradually going dark?

Joshua Johnson had been our clown, a gangly kid with an irrepressible sense of humor. "Do you *know* what Josh

*did* last night?" we'd ask each other incredulously, eager
to tell of some new stunt, a water tower climbed or a
grumpy teacher's porch festooned with toilet paper. No
one ever thought of Joshua growing up. Now he was
vice president of an insurance company, a bit heavy
around the middle, a gold chain on his graying chest.
When did that irresponsible kid's feet finally stop dancing and hit the ground? Somewhere, I thought, another
ghost of that young Josh was lying on a beach in the
sunshine, working just long enough to pay a few bills,
then taking off again for another beach, more sunshine.

And yet, as I wandered longer through the clusters
of friends, watching faces suddenly come into focus, I
wondered about how real those ghosts were. How different, indeed, might any of us have become? Dorita
McLaughlin still had her nervous laugh. How it had
irritated me then, as I had tried to talk to her about a
teenager's serious matters: changing friendships, wistful
romances, fears about the future. Dorita had listened
and laughed, turning my worries into foolishness. Eventually I stopped confiding in her. How, amazingly, that
laugh still irritated me, as I tried gently to probe into
her life now. Did she like living in Cleveland, did running a color-consultant business give her pleasure, had
she ever thought of marrying? We had known each other
for almost thirty-five years, and I felt a strange urgency
in my questions. I wanted to believe there was another
Dorita underneath that smiling mask, whose real answers hovered in the shattered aftermath of that trilling
laugh. Even in third grade, when we'd met on the school-
yard swings, Dorita had been awkward and unsure, I
recalled, even then burdened by that extra weight she
still carried. When had she decided to hide herself? Was
it so long ago that she could no longer remember? Had
another self ever had a chance to come out?

Across the room I glanced at Mark Ogilsby, who looked

much the same, towheaded, openmouthed, a little silly. But Sally, a friend who stood next to Dorita, followed my glance and said, "Have you noticed how much Mark looks like his father? He's got Mr. Ogilsby's chins now." I focused more sharply. Yes, the folds of sagging flesh did give him his father's ponderous profile, I realized; Mark, who was now a midwestern distributor for a large tool-and-die firm, suddenly merged into my memory of aging, conservative Mr. Ogilsby, the town's upright banker. All night I picked up similar murmurs: "He looks just like his old man . . . He's lost his hair, like his father . . . Now that she's older, don't Lillian's sharp features remind you of her mom?" The filaments of genetic inheritance were winding and tightening around us.

"Everyone has done so *well!*" Dorita gushed, departing for the raw veggies and dip. "Would you *believe* how suave Bobby Stone looks? Did you know he's got a houseboat in Sausalito? He's a really big deal lawyer with some posh firm and I guess he travels all over the world." Yes, I nodded, he had done well. But I had talked to Bobby earlier, and I had noticed that underneath that Italian silk suit, he still seemed somewhat shy and defensive. Perhaps because twenty-five years ago we'd had crushes on each other, though unfortunately at different times, we shared a special tenderness. I was able to ask Bobby some of the questions Dorita had turned aside, and Bobby answered. Yes, he was proud of his financial and professional success. No, he hadn't recovered from his recent divorce, and he still fought fiercely with his ex-wife. "I keep my eyes open, and I sure go out a lot, but I just can't seem to find the right woman," he said with a frustrated wince.

I wondered if Bobby were fighting his battles alone. As if he'd read my mind, Bobby said, "Just spent ten minutes talking to Willie. Did you know he sees a Jungian dream analyst? Would you have believed it? Wow."

He paused. "Well, I'm not all that surprised, Bobby," I said, a little cautiously. "I'll bet a lot of us have had some experience with therapy — whether it's straight Freudian stuff, marriage counseling, encounter groups, EST, whatever. I have. Haven't you?" He grinned widely, as if relieved. "I sure have," he said, quite cheerfully. "A female shrink, quite a terror. Four years, off and on." We smiled at each other, in silent commiseration and encouragement. But I think we both felt somehow heartened. Neither one of us had stopped hoping for changes in our lives, and we knew we were not alone. Around us, beneath all the laughter, clinking glasses, and glad cries of recognition, were people who, like us, had known silences. Dark quiet places where the hidden self darted back and forth, like a gleaming fish one only glimpsed for moments before it disappeared again in the tangled weeds and black water. In the past twenty-five years, it would have been impossible not to have visited those places, however briefly.

Maybe we returned with renewed determination. I thought of the restless energy and uncertainty many of us emanated, like a background humming, an almost unheard vibrato behind the steady melody of jobs, marriages, children, travels. We weren't ready to stop yet. We were still going places, even if the places were not as romantic or as glamorous as the ones we'd once dreamed about.

"Hey, Sue!" A loud bass voice carried across the room. I looked up and saw Sam Boles, another old friend, signaling to me from his tightly clustered group. "I'll be over in a minute," I shouted, and waved back. Startled, I realized that when Sam had called my name, I had had a strange instant of recognition. He had been calling *me*, who I was now, not all the insubstantial dream selves who had never existed. Since I had arrived here, my ghosts had somehow vanished. Perhaps after this re-

236

union, I could see them more realistically. That young woman tapping down the streets of San Francisco; the wife in a midwestern college town; the Maine innkeeper in her chamois shirt and faded jeans; all would have had to cope and adjust. Since they would all have been me, the deepest adjustments would have been the same I'd already faced. Maybe now, I thought with surprise, I'll stop watching for myself on other streets in other towns. But that doesn't mean I'm stuck where I am. It doesn't mean I'll be doing exactly the same thing when I come back to our next reunion, or that I'll look just the same either, or that I can't feel or see something differently.

"Hey," Bobby said softly, touching my arm. "Listen, I've got to go. I have to call home. But if you're not here when I get back — well, how about visiting sometime in Sausalito? I've got plenty of room for you and James. The kids would love to meet you. We'd have a great time. I'm glad you came tonight. It's been too long." I looked at Bobby. I didn't see any ghosts hovering around him either. "I'll do that," I said. I gave him a quick hug. "And I'm glad I came too."

## ABOUT THE AUTHOR

Susan Allen Toth, author of the successful *Blooming: A Small-Town Girlhood* and *Ivy Days: Making My Way Out East*, as well as stories and essays in numerous magazines, was born in 1940 in Ames, Iowa. She attended Smith College, the University of California at Berkeley, and the University of Minnesota; since 1969, she has been a member of the English Department at Macalester College. She lives with her husband, architect James Stageberg, and her daughter, Jennifer, near Lake Harriet in Minneapolis, Minnesota.